# The Essence of Soul Retrieval:
# a Shamanic Healing Practices Guide

Walter J. Cooke

Lulu.com

Copyright © 2009 by Walter John Cooke

All rights reserved. No portion of this book may be reproduced, by any process or technique, without the express prior written consent of the publisher except in the case of brief quotations embodied in critical articles and reviews or where permitted by law. For further information please contact the publisher at the address listed below.

The information in this book is for educational purposes. The author and publishers are in no way liable for any use or misuse of the information.

The core shamanic method of healing that is described in this book should not be considered an exclusive means of dealing with medical issues. Shamanic healing practices should be seen as complementary or alternative ways to augment regular allopathic medical or psychological treatment, unless contrary medical advice is given.

Library of Congress Control Number: 2009903478
Cooke, Walter. 1952-
   The Essence of Soul Retrieval: a Shamanic Healing Practices Guide / Walter Cooke
      p.   cm.
   Includes bibliographical references and index.
   ISBN 978-0-557-06166-2

Second revised and expanded edition published in 2009 by:
Lulu.com
860 Aviation Parkway, Suite 300
Morrisville, NC 27560
USA
www.lulu.com

Book cover artwork and all inside page artwork is copyright © 2007 by Tracey Ann Wong. All rights reserved. Used with permission.

Material from Soul Retrieval Newsletter is copyright © 1990 by Sandra Ingerman. All rights reserved. Used with permission.

The paper used in this book complies with the Permanent Paper Standard issued by the National Information Standards Organization (Z39.48-1984).

V2.104_P21-APR-09

# The Essence of Soul Retrieval:
# a Shamanic Healing Practices Guide

Second Revised and Expanded Edition
Copyright © 2009 by Walter J. Cooke. All rights reserved.

## *Medical Disclaimer*

Medical disclaimers may appear to insult the intelligence and common sense of both the practitioner and client using complementary and alternative forms of health care. Such disclaimers may also reduce the potential benefits of energy medicine, calling into question the efficacy of shamanic practices and casting doubt into the minds of those seeking potential ways of self-empowerment and alternative means of healing themselves. That said, the following information is for general information purposes only, with the user accepting all responsibility for applying the information presented. Energetic healing systems such as shamanism are commonly considered as complementary therapies to sanctioned medical or psychological treatments. Spiritual practitioners are not authorized to diagnose or treat medical or psychological illness. In such cases, clients and practitioners are advised to contact a licensed health professional.

## *Audience*

This book is a reference guide for learning and performing the shamanic practice of soul retrieval. It assumes that you have already completed detailed work in core shamanic practices, including: shamanic journeying, working with the Helping Spirits, doing a vision quest, retrieving power animals, contacting spirit guides to assist you in your work, and facilitating energy healing work. Experience that includes empowerment and self-knowledge gained from healing one's own soul, through both group and individual spiritual practices, is also an important foundation. If you have not undertaken these activities then you probably still need to do some preparation for this new work. Please keep this book for future reference when you feel ready to perform this vocation.

Shamanic work requires physical, emotional, mental and spiritual action and understanding in order to properly carry out the craft. Soul retrieval work is best learned as part of a comprehensive shamanic practices program, done under the tutelage of a shaman who is well practiced in teaching soul retrieval. Please honestly assess your current abilities and remedy any weak areas before returning back to this book for instruction on the techniques of soul retrieval. This work is not the place for ego inflation and self-importance – it is done with humility, wisdom, and trust that Love and Spirit heal the wounds of the soul, not the frail power of human will or ego's desire.

## *Acknowledgements*

The author would like to thank everyone, named and unnamed, who have helped make this book possible. Martha Lucier contributed both her wisdom and experience in teaching soul retrieval; without her guidance and example this book could not have been envisioned or created. Thank you, Martha. Also, Sandra Ingerman's books and newsletters on soul retrieval are the 'gold standard' for illuminating this ancient art in modern form, and giving compassionate advice to both practitioners and those seeking this form of healing. Thank you for all your contributions to this important work, Sandra.

Professor Leslie E. Korn, Ph.D., M.P.H., R.P.P. of Union Institute & University, the Center for Traditional Medicine, and the Center for World Indigenous Studies, provided critical insight and encouragement to ensure this work met the University's academic standards while still offering me the opportunity to spread my wings and explore new territory.

My circle of companions in the shamanic way, with whom I have shared an amazing journey over the past years, all deserve kudos for their courage, curiosity and camaraderie. My appreciation to Bill, Diane, Emily, Jen, Julie, Keith, Kim, Maria, Martha, Monika, Peter, Ronda, Swahaama, Tara, Tom, Trae, and Will. We may not have all made it to the end of our program together, but we are all still present in spirit. Each of you contributed many personal insights and are all truly beautiful beings, assisting me in the discovery of my own path with heart.

A very special thank you goes to Tracey Ann Wong for generously allowing me to use her beautiful and inspiring artwork on the cover and throughout the book.

I am grateful to Gail, Maria and Jennifer for text reviews and photographic support. Thanks also to Alain Herriott, a great creative spirit at Quantum-Touch™, for his perceptive contributions concerning belief systems, energy acuity and energy healing processes.

Extra special thanks go to the Helping Spirits and especially to The Ancient Muse for their loving, gentle, timeless urging towards knowing, making visible the implicate order.

# Contents

| | |
|---|---|
| MEDICAL DISCLAIMER | I |
| AUDIENCE | I |
| ACKNOWLEDGEMENTS | II |
| CONTENTS | V |
| | |
| **FOREWORD** | **1** |
| | |
| **PREFACE** | **3** |
| | |
| **INTRODUCTION** | **5** |
| | |
| **SECTION ONE – THE LIFE OF THE SOUL** | **13** |
| | |
| AN INTRODUCTION TO THE LIFE OF THE SOUL | 13 |
| THE PROCESS OF SOUL RETRIEVAL | 16 |
| | |
| **SECTION TWO – PREPARATION AND PAPERWORK** | **21** |
| | |
| INITIAL CLIENT CONTACT | 21 |
| ETHICAL CONSIDERATIONS | 26 |
| SETTING UP SACRED SPACE | 30 |
| BECOMING THE HOLLOW BONE | 32 |
| | |
| **SECTION THREE – THE CORE PROCESS** | **37** |

| | |
|---|---|
| **LOVE, NOT TECHNIQUE** | 37 |
| **INITIAL PRACTITIONER PREPARATION** | 38 |
| **CLIENT PREPARATION FOR THE JOURNEY** | 39 |
| **MAKING ROOM** | 41 |
| **THE SOUL RETRIEVAL JOURNEY** | 42 |
| **TRACKING THE SOUL ESSENCE** | 43 |
| **RETRIEVING THE SOUL ESSENCE** | 44 |
| **RETURNING AND RESTORING THE SOUL ESSENCE** | 50 |
| **COMPLETING THE WORK** | 57 |
| **JOURNEYING FOR A HEALING STORY** | 61 |
| **SHARING THE SOUL RETRIEVAL JOURNEY** | 64 |
| **WHAT IS A 'HEALING STORY?'** | 67 |
| **THEFT OF SOUL ESSENCE FROM OTHERS** | 68 |
| **MARTHA'S SOUL RETRIEVAL REMINDERS FOR LEARNERS** | 69 |
| **OTHER TIPS FOR LEARNERS TO REMEMBER** | 70 |

## SECTION FOUR – CLIENT SUPPORT                                          73

| | |
|---|---|
| **SUPPORT AND FOLLOW-UP** | 73 |
| **CLIENT RECOVERY, HEALING CRISIS, SPIRITUAL BYPASS** | 75 |

## SECTION FIVE – ADVANCED TOPICS                                         79

| | |
|---|---|
| **OTHER TYPES OF SOUL RETRIEVAL** | 79 |
| **ALTERNATIVE METHODS FOR DOING SOUL RETRIEVAL** | 80 |
| **OPENING TO A MORE COMPLETE SELF** | 81 |
| **EMPOWERING YOUR WORK** | 84 |
| **GUIDED VISUALIZATION** | 85 |
| **BODY POSITIONS TO AUGMENT YOUR JOURNEY** | 86 |

| | |
|---|---|
| PRACTITIONER BURNOUT AND HOW TO AVOID IT | 90 |
| THE DELICATE SUBJECT OF PAYMENT FOR YOUR SERVICES | 92 |

## LAST THOUGHTS: SPIRITUAL AID AND THE NEEDS OF STRANGERS — 95

| | |
|---|---|
| LIVING OUR DREAM WITH POWER AND INTENTION | 95 |
| FEEDBACK | 97 |

## SOURCES AND FURTHER READINGS — 99

## ANNEX — 105

| | |
|---|---|
| INITIAL CONTACT MESSAGE | 105 |
| CLIENT INTAKE FORM | 107 |
| CLIENT INTERACTION FORMS | 108 |
| FOLLOW-UP AFTER THE SOUL RETRIEVAL | 110 |
| TEACHING A PERSON HOW TO JOURNEY | 111 |
| NOTES ON PERFORMING ENERGY EXTRACTION WORK | 114 |

## ABOUT THE AUTHOR — 129

*Dedicated to my parents, Alma and Walter.*

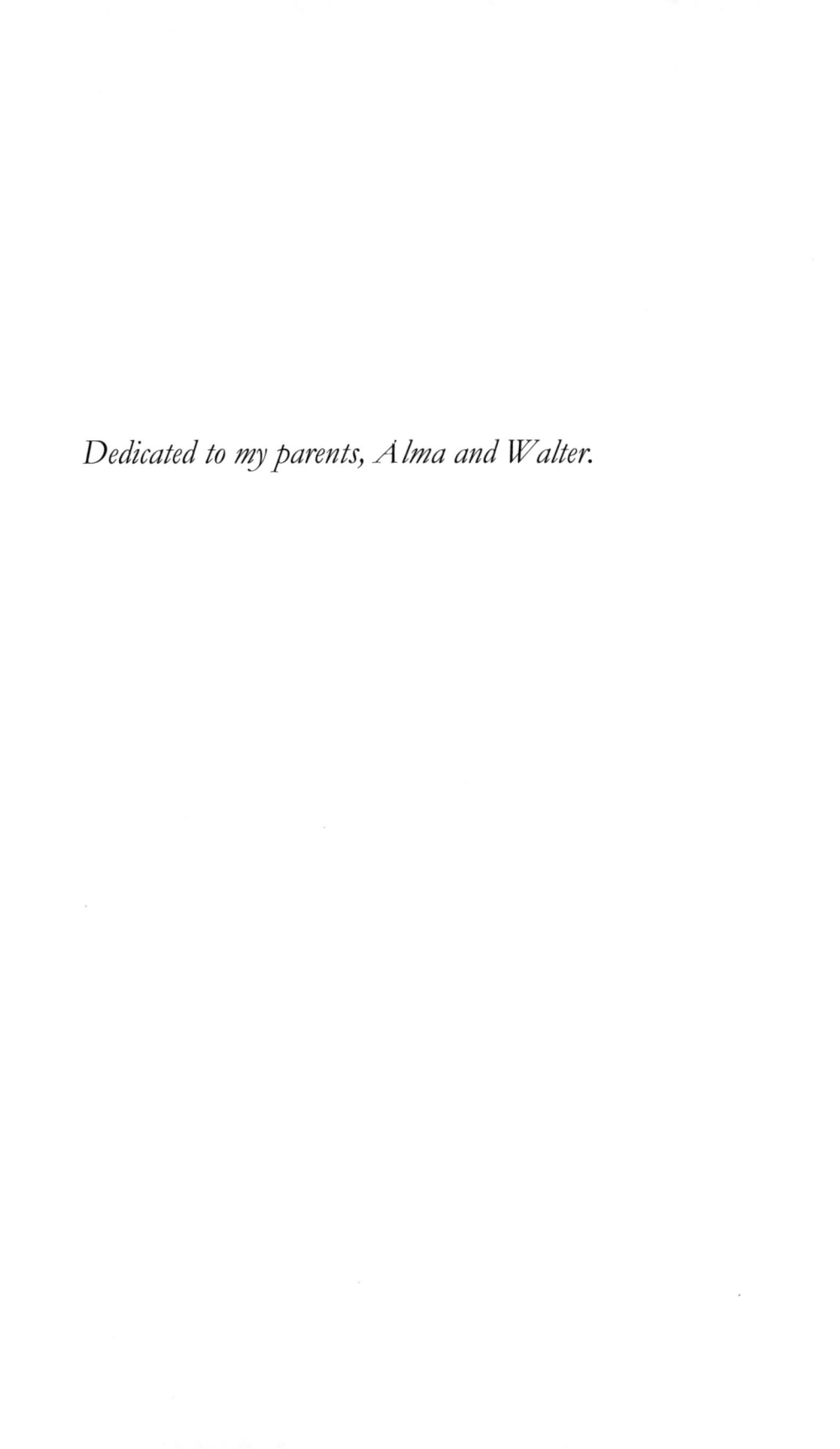

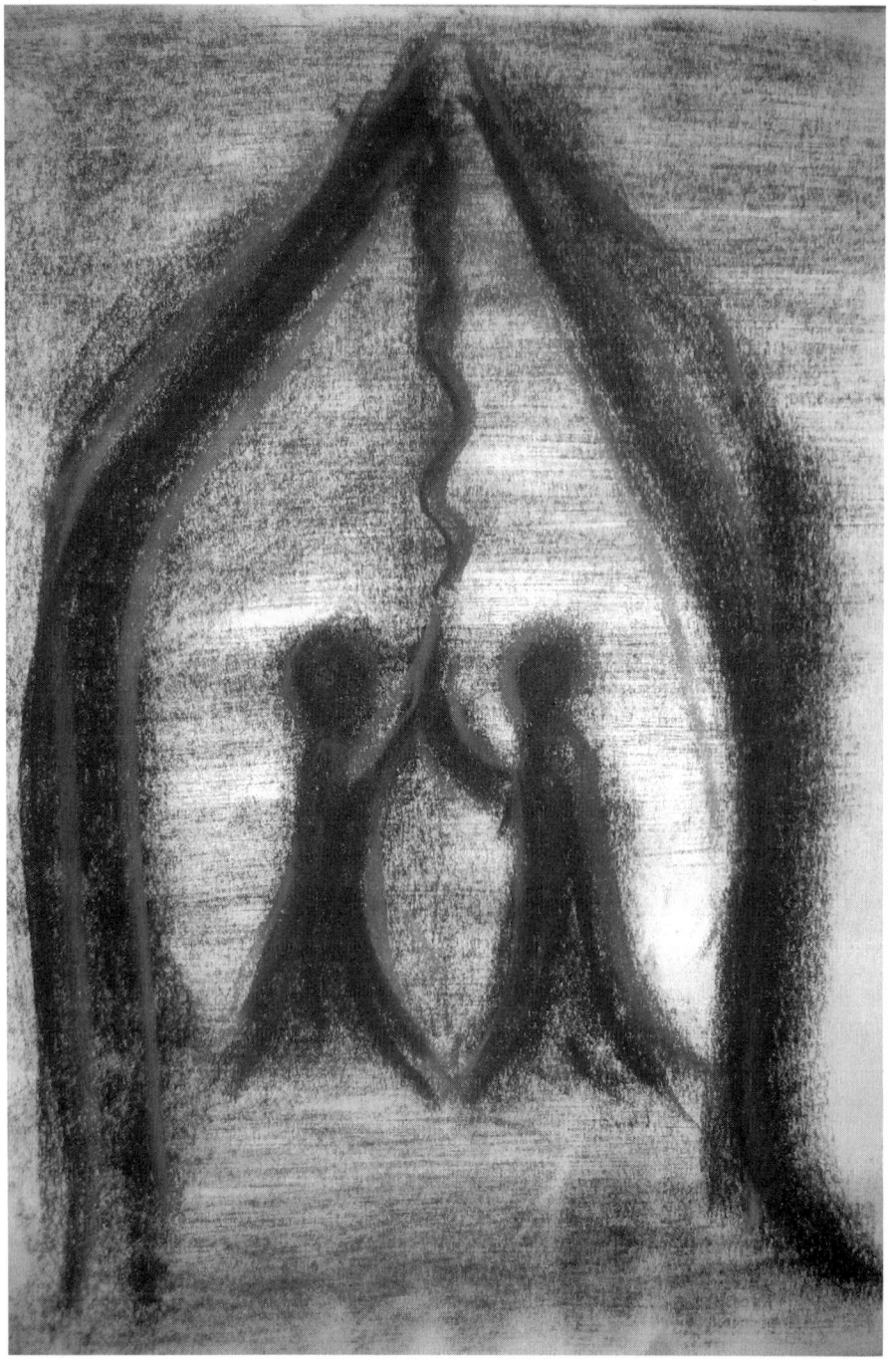

# Foreword

The practice of shamanism is as old as human-kind. Yet the knowledge and wisdom of shamanic practices, having passed through millennia bound within an oral and experiential tradition offered only to a select few, is now available to the many. Thus this book signals a nodal shift in the transfer of knowledge and the potential for energy exchange among many clients and practitioners; the written words of Walter Cooke elucidate a practical approach to shamanic practices that are designed to be shared and practiced with a guide trained in the ancient traditions for modern application.

It is no small feat to put into language, that which is ineffable – that which shifts shape as often as it may be recognizably grabbed or held. Yet this step-by-step guide thoughtfully and ethically instructs the reader to explore consciousness and travel realms with guides who are present to facilitate healing and wisdom. Shamanic practice is about the transcendence of the limitations normally associated with earthly, material boundaries. Still, as human-animals we are designed to transmute and return again and again, applying lessons learned.

I have guided many hundreds of individuals over the last 35 years; patients, students, educators, and healers, many who sought to retrieve and restore their soul to its rightful place within the whole being. There is no greater journey that can be undertaken, either as a guide or the guided, for it is the foundation of a purposeful and compassionate life. By writing this book, Walter has brought to life the wisdom of his teacher. He thus joins the ranks of those who share, with humility, their gifts, so that others may express, find and retrieve their own.

This book is a must for any library of the serious shamanic practitioner, as well as for the novice beginning her or his journey. You will doubtless take your first journey and return again and again with this book by your side. Take this next important step on your own path of self-discovery; after all, you are holding it now for a reason.

Leslie Korn, PhD, MPH
Director, Center for Traditional Medicine
Olympia, WA, USA

# Preface

Once upon a time, long before anyone can re-member, the Creator gave birth to Earth. It began as a heart that pulsed, like a human heart floating in space while spinning and sharing its beauty.

With each pulse a new creation was woven around the heart like a beautiful tapestry of vibrant colour. With one pulse the oceans were created, with another the mighty forests, and yet another the magnificent mountains and valleys, and so on and so on. While spinning, the Earth shared Her beauty and joy for all.

The Mystery of the Universe admired the beauty of the Earth through the stars – the eyes of the universe. The Creator longed to be on the Earth to experience the Earth's exquisite beauty. With this intention, while looking upon the Earth, sparks of light began to fall from the stars in the form of humans. And so it would be that humans would carry the spark of the Creator in their own hearts while engaging all of their senses to experience life at its fullest upon the Earth.

## The Essence of Soul Retrieval

Many millennia later, a young child named 'Innocence' skipped along a forested path admiring the Earth's beauty. A shadowy figure jumped out of the dark bush, frightening her. Not having had this experience before, she wove an invisible cloak around her to protect the light within her heart, for her heart carried her most precious gift, that of *All of Creation*. Each time Innocence came upon something that was unknown to her or that she feared, she wove a new layer of protection around her heart.

Eventually, the light within the heart of Innocence became so protected and dulled that she forgot it was there. She forgot who she was, her life purpose, and what it was she came to this planet to experience. She was unaware that the shadow that came to her was really a way for her to experience the light within, for without darkness we cannot know our light.

The role of the Shaman is to awaken us from our slumber, Re-Calling our essence and our beauty, so that we may Re-Member who we are and why we came to this earthly plane. Walter has captured the essence of the practice of soul retrieval through this book, reminding us that it is love and compassion that heals, along with the assistance of the Helping Spirits who support us in our healing process.

May we all return to our Innocence remembering our brilliance, beauty and magnificence within.

Martha Lucier – BHk, BEd
Co-founder, Northern Edge Algonquin Retreat and Awareness Centre
South River, Ontario, Canada

# Introduction

The ancient practice of soul retrieval is one of the most powerful healing processes that you will learn while walking the shamanic path with heart. In this book you will learn the formal process carried out by modern core shamanic practitioners to retrieve the lost soul essence of a person, with effective reintegration, so the client may heal the deepest wounds of their soul.

The results you will see after performing soul retrieval work can include subtle, deep and spectacular changes for the recipient. I performed a soul retrieval restoring the essence a client lost when she was forced to write with her right hand at the age of seven. Retrieving the energy lost from this trauma enabled her to begin expressing her missing artistic side and, at the age of 48, she began to draw and paint (using her left hand). I received a profound soul retrieval that permitted resolution and healing of emotional trauma from a lifetime 1200 years ago. Everyone is different. Some people may take many months to integrate the soul essence that is returned, while others have immediate 'fireworks' with this newly recovered power that can surprise, delight and frighten.

As well as learning the formal process of soul retrieval, additional resources and tips are provided from the experience of fellow practitioners. These resources will ease the journey for you, helping you avoid some of the more common pitfalls that may be encountered. And, as time goes by, you can periodically refer back to this book if the steps get a bit hazy or you find yourself looking for tips to deal with something that may not have been covered in the basic course work with your personal teacher. Later, when you decide to stretch your wings and soar a bit higher, there are some advanced techniques and suggestions for you to explore on your own.

Spirit once told me during a shamanic journey that healing work is linked with the sacred concept of *kairikai* (pronounced: "<u>care</u>-a-kye"): a qualitative sense of being in the right place at the right time with the right tools and the right intention. *Everything* had to be present and properly aligned or the desired spiritual healing outcome would not be attained. I subsequently learned that there is an archaic Greek word representing one of the qualitative aspects of time in ancient Greek culture – *kairos* (καιρός, nominative masculine, 2nd. declension) – that embodies some of the meaning in this 'moment of perfect alignment.'

The ancient art of soul retrieval requires more than learning a set procedure that you blindly follow. This book does provide a set of basic steps for you to follow when you are initially learning how to perform soul retrieval. However, as you become more comfortable with the practice, you will quickly find that things are a lot more flexible in terms

# Introduction

of how you proceed at each step along the way. All shamanic practices require the use of spirit to accomplish the work. What the term spirit means here is all of the material and immaterial forms of conscious energy that surround us. Your mindful intention for each shamanic journey asks the Helping Spirits to direct and inform your work. The Helping Spirits respond with information and guidance you need during the soul retrieval process. While the shamanic practitioner is meticulous in thought and action, he or she is paradoxically totally flexible in thought and deed, as guidance is received from Spirit.

Soul retrieval requires many steps: preparatory work for both you and your client, journeying to your Helping Spirits for advice, setting proper intention, creating the sacred space for the soul retrieval, journeying to locate and retrieve the lost soul essence, and follow-up work performed afterwards to help your client realign with this soul energy and fully integrate it back into their life. No small task! However, with Spirit's help and meticulous attention to this principle of *kairikai*, you will be more assured of having the best possible outcome.

Several prominent authors have written about the experience of soul retrieval, including Sandra Ingerman and Alberto Villoldo. Their popular works help the layman to understand what it is and why one might want to embark on the soul retrieval journey. However, what is missing is a step-by-step guide that supports the shamanic practitioner in learning how to do the actual work. That is why this book was written.

To guide you through the full process, this book is divided into five sections: an introduction to the life of the soul, preparations that you and your client need to do before retrieving soul essence, learning the soul retrieval core process, a client follow-up section to detail the client's life journey after the formal soul retrieval process has been completed, and an advanced topics section for other areas of soul retrieval not normally covered by an instructor. Some instructors believe our Helping Spirits have all the information and we do not really need a shamanic teacher. Those who are called to the work will discern a preferred way to learn and practice, either alone or with help.

Section One – The Life of the Soul explores what we mean when we talk about soul, spirit, and the process of soul retrieval. What is 'soul loss' and why do we need a process to bring back lost soul essence? Why is a shamanic practitioner the best person to perform this type of work and what training is required? To introduce the sections that follow, the entire soul retrieval process is outlined for you in a step-by-step manner.

Section Two – Preparations and Paperwork covers the preparatory steps completed in the days leading up to the actual soul retrieval. As with every important job that is correctly done, soul retrieval is generally '90% preparation and 10% perspiration' to do the core soul retrieval process. When time has been taken to properly set the stage and prepare your client for this life-changing event, the actual core work is usually very easy and beneficial results are more likely to be achieved.

It is critically important to involve the client in their own healing work, to immerse them in a space where they are open to taking responsibility for their own healing. After all, it is the client who is the 'healer,' not the shamanic practitioner. 'A healer' is someone who was sick and then got better. 'Great healers' are just those who were very ill and still managed to return themselves to health once again. As a shamanic

## Introduction

practitioner we are only the conduit – 'the hollow bone' – that Spirit operates through. We also generally embody the archetype of 'the wounded healer' – those who, from the depths of their own personal illnesses, have explored what it means to heal him or her self. We are often the ones best suited to help others on their own healing journey. In Section Two this interaction between practitioner and healer is explored in depth.

Section Three – The Core Process takes the student through the entire soul retrieval process of final preparations, meeting with the client and carrying out the shamanic journey to retrieve the lost soul essence for the client. Much interaction will occur between you, the client, and Spirit during this work, so considerable attention is focused on this section, including some of the potential interactions while working in Non-Ordinary Reality (NOR). This information can be especially helpful to the beginner, providing some idea of what may be experienced while performing a soul retrieval and how you can best work on your client's behalf while retrieving their lost soul essence in NOR.

Section Four – Client Follow-up tracks the work required after the formal soul retrieval is complete. To properly integrate the recovered soul energy, the client must make room for this energy in their life. Prompt follow-up with the client will help to ensure that they continue with their healing work and develop a relationship with their recovered essence, even if this involves an unexpected 'healing crisis.' A healing crisis can manifest in the form of physical and emotional release that the client is unfamiliar with. When a client has difficulty integrating the returned soul essence, the practitioner's active intervention can assist in defusing this crisis and accelerate the healing process.

Section Five – Advanced Topics introduces other types of soul retrieval beyond the most common work you will do with individuals. It explores alternative ways of performing soul retrieval, and describes techniques from shamanism and other energy medicine modalities that can be used to further empower your soul retrieval practice. Problems such as practitioner burnout (and how to avoid it), and the delicate issue of deciding how to be paid for your services are also discussed.

Last Thoughts: Spiritual Aid and the Needs of Strangers considers our work in its larger context. How is the role of the shamanic practitioner changing over time and how does this influence our community and the world at large? Does 'walking the path with heart' put us in a better position to act impeccably in an increasingly complex world?

The Sources and Annex sections provide information on other resources, sample text and teaching material for developing your own unique practice. For example, there are emails that illustrate how to guide your preparations with the client, and an outline for teaching a client to journey in NOR if they are unfamiliar with this healing process.

The preparation and depth of the journeys done on behalf of the client may appear daunting to many students approaching this work for the first time. However, do not forget that Spirit is actually doing the work. You are setting the stage and helping the client to manifest the results. It is through the gift of your loving support and a deep desire to help them recover soul energy that was lost through trauma, which assists in returning them to a place of balance and wellness. The journey is

## Introduction

actually very exciting and many shamanic practitioners feel filled with ecstasy while they are retrieving lost soul essence for their client. It is a profound and numinous experience, well worth the effort to learn how to perform. You will also have special power animals and Helping Spirits to call on for guidance and support during the soul retrieval journey – it is not done alone. And so, under the tutelage of your shamanic teacher, you are now ready to undertake a very exciting step on your own individual path with heart.

*"In the human body all the secrets of the universe are expressed. The human body is a true microcosm, and when speaking through it, the human soul, manifesting its own inner life, can make visible in artistic form all secrets of the universe."*

— Rudolf Steiner

# Section One – The Life of the Soul

## *An Introduction to the Life of the Soul*

Removing the usual religious beliefs from its meaning, let us imagine *the soul* as being the vital living quintessence of who we have been, who we are at this moment, and who we will evolve into in the time to come. This definition implies that our inner life force, core being and essential qualities are all a part of our soul. Our soul is bound to, but also expands beyond our physical body, ego, and mortality. The soul connects us to our present time and space, yet also radiates beyond our consciousness to access the infinite intelligence of what psychologist Carl Jung called the personal and collective unconscious. Our 'spirit' is our perfect god/goddess nature that stays the same, while our 'soul' evolves over time.

However, there are times when we suffer trauma that injures our body, psyche and soul. 'Soul loss' is a survival mechanism – it is how we endure trauma. This trauma may be a result of physical pain from something like a car accident, psychological stress from what is experienced in conditions of war, or some form of personal violence or deeply felt grief. In these types of circumstances, our psyche tries to protect itself by disassociating from the trauma, and a part of our essence leaves us rather than remaining to experience the pain. People who have undergone such extreme forms of trauma are normally labeled by the medical community as suffering from 'PTSD' – Post Traumatic Stress Disorder. Shamanic practitioners refer to this situation as being in a state of soul loss.

The symptoms of soul loss can include: feeling empty as though one is observing life instead of living it, numbness, apathy, chronic depression, depleted immune system, chronic illness, memory gaps, addictions, Dissociative Identity Disorder, or emotional difficulty moving on after the death of a loved one or a divorce. When a person says "I've never felt the same since the time I…" or "I don't feel like I'm experiencing the world, I'm only watching it from a detached point of view," or other similar observations, then they are relating the experience of living with soul loss. Using the process of psychotherapy, a therapist might determine that the cause of a person's depression or addiction is a neurosis or complex in the person's psyche brought on by trauma; a shaman will simply say that the cause is soul loss.

Some shamanic practitioners believe the process of psychotherapy is imperfect as initial treatment for those who have suffered trauma. In

## Section One – The Life of the Soul

her 1991 book on soul retrieval, psychologist and practicing shaman Sandra Ingerman states: "… experience has shown me that psychotherapy only works on the parts of us that are 'home.' If a vital part of our essence has fled, how can we bring it back?" She continues: "… for the soul to be explored, it has to be in residence. How well can psychotherapy succeed when the therapist is talking to a person who isn't home?"

To survive trauma, a soul part flees to the protection of Pachamama, the Spirit Mother in the Lower World. To retrieve a lost soul part, a shaman journeys in non-ordinary reality, retrieving the lost life energy and reintegrating it back into the soul so it is again accessible to the individual. Until this is done, the individual remains in a state of soul loss, feeling as though some part of them is missing or that a part of their vital life energy has been split off and is unavailable. Our primary work with soul retrieval (SR) is to help a client heal the individual traumas of their past by retrieving only the soul essence or energy that was lost during these events. It is important to understand that SR returns pure essence that was lost, not the traumatized part of the person's psyche. We are not asking the client to re-experience the original trauma in order to recover the lost energy – they need only be open to receiving the energy that rightfully already belongs to them.

Medical intuitive Caroline Myss believes that this energy is not 'lost,' rather it is 'stuck' in the past time when the traumatic stress occurred. Because these missing parts of us are caught in different 'time zones,' these particular life energies are unavailable to us in the present. From a shamanic perspective soul essence can be stuck in the middle, lower or upper worlds, outside of time and space. Whatever metaphor or framework you use to describe the trauma of soul loss, the purpose of soul retrieval is to find and reintegrate this vital life essence back into our self. This in turn makes us feel more whole, alive, and able to live our life to its fullest potential.

The information in this book is to be used to perform soul retrieval on adults. Working with children is a slightly different matter – soul retrieval can certainly be done for children and those with special needs or limited life experience. However it involves training with an experienced shaman and an approach that uses simpler metaphoric language to communicate concepts the client can better understand.

## *The process of Soul Retrieval*

This book covers the core process of performing soul retrieval. It also provides background information on other issues and requirements to be familiar with as an integral part of doing the work. The core process you study for doing the actual retrieval is obviously the most important piece to learn and practice. However, there are a number of other essential requirements surrounding the core SR work that you must also know, such as: client intake, follow-up, compassionate action and impeccable communications between yourself and the client. This book covers the basics for getting started and some of the issues and questions that will inevitably arise once you begin applying what you have learned. By conscientiously following these suggestions you may well avoid many

## Section One – The Life of the Soul

of the problems that other practitioners have encountered and so help ensure a positive soul retrieval experience.

At the same time, each person who learns and applies this work will develop his or her own unique style. Your personal development will be supported by guidance from the Helping Spirits and your own intuitive strengths as your comfort level increases. However, the core soul retrieval process generally always includes the following basic steps:

1) An initial communication from the potential client seeking assistance;
2) The shamanic practitioner gathers some preliminary information on the client and what issues they are concerned with;
3) The practitioner journeys on the client's behalf to confirm whether they and their Helping Spirits can be of assistance to the client at this time;
4) Depending on the response of the Helping Spirits, the practitioner will proceed with the process or refer the client to another individual who may be more suited to working with them;
5) The practitioner will do some client intake work, gather some basic information, and discuss the client's issues in more detail through a series of reflexive questions of self-discovery;
6) The client can be taught how to journey in order to assist in their own soul retrieval work and facilitate their own healing;
7) Practitioner and client will agree on the time and place for doing the soul retrieval work;
8) A journey to your Helping Spirits is done in preparation for performing the actual SR work to learn what you need to know in order to best do the SR work for this client;

9) The practitioner prepares the space to be used for the SR;
10) The practitioner and client meet for the soul retrieval work;
11) The practitioner clearly explains the SR process, so that the client knows what to expect, feels safe about what will transpire, and trusts in what the practitioner is going to accomplish;
12) The client may be asked to do some individual work in preparation for the soul retrieval;
13) After opening sacred space, the practitioner does the core soul retrieval work, journeying to the Lower World to find and return the lost soul essence (this may also include other preparatory journeying or energy extraction work);
14) The practitioner welcomes back the returned soul part(s) and allows time for the client to center and ground by having them reconnect with nature *before* relating any information about the journey;
15) During or after the client's time in nature, the practitioner journeys to receive a healing story for the client;
16) Using healing words, the practitioner tells the client relevant facts that are appropriate to disclose about the retrieval work, and presents the healing story;
17) The client is given time to relate their own experience, and to ask any questions requiring clarification about what happened;
18) The client is encouraged to integrate the new energy essence that has been retrieved, gain further insight, and to do follow-up work with either the shamanic practitioner or their own personal medical and psychological professionals, as they feel appropriate;

19) Before leaving, the client can offer an exchange in whatever way is preferred to recompense the practitioner for the services received;
20) The practitioner will follow-up with the client to ensure that the client is comfortable with the SR integration work, and assist them if they encounter a 'healing crisis' afterwards.

The following chapters lead you through the procedures involved in each of the above-mentioned steps.

*For today only,*

*Do not anger,*

*Do not worry,*

*Be humble,*

*Be honest in your work,*

*Be compassionate to yourself and others.*

— Mikao Usui, *Reiki Precepts*

# Section Two – Preparation and Paperwork

## *Initial Client Contact*

When a potential client contacts you seeking assistance, it is important to 'do your homework' and properly set the stage before initiating a soul retrieval. People may also contact you on behalf of others who are ill in hospital or otherwise unable to communicate by themselves. However, we must **always** have the permission of a client before doing soul retrieval work. In cases where the client cannot speak, such as an animal or baby or someone in a coma, you can journey to the middle world to ask them for their permission. If permission is unclear, journey to ask what the ethical action is for you to take in this situation. Even when the client has approached you and specifically requested your help, it is still important to journey and ask your Helping Spirits if both they and you are the right agents to assist this client in this particular circumstance. For this reason, and before proceeding further, it is best to first gather some very general information about the client and their needs and tell them you will get back to them after meditation on this issue. If your gut instincts and your Helping Spirits both agree that you can be of assistance to this new client, then it is time to do some initial preparation. If, instead, you receive a 'no,' then you need to say this to the client without causing trauma. You can, with diplomacy, simply tell them that you are not the best person to assist them at this time and refer them back to their regular health care professional or another practitioner, as deemed most appropriate.

When interviewing people, you need to ask what their current issue is and what is bothering them. Find out what is not working in their life, rather than asking for specific information about their past history and trauma. We often get both positive and negative labels attached to us by external authority figures and institutions that we deal with, including doctors and psychologists. Do not simply accept a client's definition of their 'psychological label.' These psychological labels apply to our modern medical world; in shamanic practice we want to work on *a person's individual issue*, not on a label. For example, Sandra Ingerman says that if a person comes to her and says they want a soul retrieval because they believe they are an incest survivor, she does not automatically accept that as the information she needs from the client. Instead, she wants to know what is not working in their life right now that gives them the feeling that they need soul retrieval. Her suggestion is that you work on the life problem, not on the label, because we want to see each of our clients as unique human beings and not just as labels.

## Section Two – Preparation and Paperwork

At the same time, it is important not to *invalidate* what someone says about him or herself. Instead, try to find a way to reorient your information gathering questions to reframe the client's perspective about her or his situation and their response to your queries. Offer them a new way of seeing themselves and their issue. Reiterating and summarizing what the client says by stating, "what I hear you saying is …" also tells the person that they have been clearly heard and respected. At the same time you have the opportunity to move conversation away from labeling and into the experience of the person's life in the present moment. This requires considerable tact and sensitivity on your part, so it is worth spending some time reading about the symptoms and types of trauma you are likely to encounter so that 'you will know it when you hear it.' It is very useful to consult with a mentor or supervisor for any complex issues and questions that arise. A practicing shaman or therapist can support you with advice and assistance if you feel uncomfortable with a developing situation or feelings concerning a client. Seek additional support when you feel unclear or 'out of your depth' with the work.

There are some basic questions that you can give a new client to think about and respond to. This can be a printed form you give them or an email that you send for their written response. Some clients may want to speak to you on the telephone rather than providing you with written responses. Try to accommodate the preferences of the client and their preferred mode of communications when asking for information. Some forms, adapted from Martha Lucier's basic intake communications, can be tailored for your own paper or email exchanges and are provided in the Annex at the end of this book.

Basic queries to ask the client include:

Please share what you are comfortable relating to me about why you feel you need a soul retrieval.

What is not working for you in your life right now?

What do you hope to gain from this experience?

What do you believe will be different after the soul retrieval?

What are you prepared to do to help integrate the retrieved soul essence into your life?

What other therapists or support persons are in your life now who can assist you going forward in the work you want to do?

You will want to supplement these with other insightful questions as you become more familiar with the work and your own requirements, emphasizing what you think is useful for the client to reflect on when preparing for soul retrieval. For example, you may also want to determine what medications they are currently taking, if they are under medical care, and the names of their doctors, therapists, and any other health care practitioners who are working with them and what treatments are involved. Some clients may not be open to sharing this information with you. Ideally, clients will indicate they have a supporting therapist or similar practitioner in the consent and liability release forms. Journey and ask for applicable questions that are most relevant to each particular client.

You will also want to offer some background information and a description of the SR process to the client, satisfying their desire to feel comfortable with what is being proposed. This also invites their involvement in the healing process. Let your intuition guide you as to how much or how little you disclose about the procedure, possibly providing a short description of the general process that does not include overly esoteric jargon or potentially frightening concepts for the ordinary person. Sandra Ingerman provides good SR overviews for clients in her soul retrieval books. Find one that you like and memorize it.

The responses from the client will help you determine how to proceed with the work. Does the person sound sincere in their desire to bring more of their essence and spirit back into their life? Are they just doing this because it sounds like a cool thing that one of their friends did? What is their relationship to the sacred in their everyday life? Finally, does the client sound like they are psychologically healthy and willing to assimilate this soul energy into their psyche? Review all of the information you gather, and then journey with the intention of seeking advice on whether the Helping Spirits will work with you and this client for this SR. It may be that someone else is better suited to facilitate this client's work. Do not take it personally if the Helping Spirits say "no," as you may not be aware of some important facts. Have a diplomatic way of saying no to the client that will avoid causing them any trauma or embarrassment.

'Difficult' clients will appear, possibly presenting psychological or physical challenges to your normal way of working with people. You are under no obligation to work with a potential client. Only take on cases that you feel comfortable handling. People with severe physical or psychological problems may be better helped using traditional allopathic medicine or psychotherapy. Psychotic and schizophrenic people can appear to suffer from 'spirit possession' or energetic intrusions. It can be a challenge to determine their ability to work with you and also for them to

## The Essence of Soul Retrieval

journey in non-ordinary reality. Make certain that you feel safe; have another person present who can assist you and help ensure safety.

In certain circumstances, soul retrieval may not be what is needed. For example, in cases of spirit possession the services of a psychopomp may be more appropriate. If the situation seems confusing, one gifted shaman physician and psychotherapist noted that "if the voices the person hears are closer than the person's shoulder, then they are suffering from spirit possession; if the voices speaking to them are from their shoulder outwards, then they are suffering a psychosis and need more traditional professional care from the medical community."

Before meeting the client, journey with the intention of finding out what you need to know in order to perform this particular soul retrieval. You may be given specific information to prepare special resources needed for working with this client. Pay close attention to your intuition and any synchronicities indicating what you might or might not do in preparation.

## *Ethical Considerations*

There are also important ethical considerations to remember when working with clients. "Do no harm" is a good motto to keep in mind. Always maintain personal and professional boundaries with clients. You are *not* going to be their new best friend or sexual partner! Sexual contact will be destructive to both party's wellbeing and is absolutely inappropriate in all circumstances. Appropriate boundaries and protocols have to be in place to emphasize the protection of physical, psychological and personal ego boundaries. You must be knowledgeable and consciously aware of the psychological processes of projection, transference and counter-transference that can and will occur between practitioner and client. Be especially mindful of projections where you become a mirror for someone. Clients can be vulnerable and may see you as a powerful archetypal figure who will 'save them' during their dark night of the soul. You, in turn, may be drawn to act out your own psyche's shadow material and play the role of 'wounded healer' or 'savior.' Read a basic psychology book if you are not familiar with these concepts. Carl Jung's Collected Works can be a rather intimidating place for the layman to begin; fortunately there are a number of authors who have clarified and expanded on his groundbreaking work. *Projection and Re-Collection in Jungian Psychology* by Marie-Louise von Franz is an excellent book for exploring the subject of projection, while *The Essential Jung* by Anthony Storr provides an overview of important areas of psychology, including transference and counter-transference.

One way to help ensure your interactions with clients are seen as being beyond reproach is to always work with an assistant present – someone who can witness and assist you by scribing and drumming. This is especially important when male practitioners are working with female clients – having a female assistant present will both help the client feel safe and limit the client's capacity to 'act out' their transference material. Both you and your client want to feel safe and not vulnerable to any unintentional misunderstandings in your interactions. It is *strongly suggested* that you to have the proper structure in place to support a safe and protective environment for everyone.

Everything that transpires between you and your client remains confidential. The sacred container that you (and your assistant, drummer, or other helpers present) work inside acts as a protective barrier against the outside world, letting the client know that this place is different from the life and trauma they experience 'out there.' This sacred container also symbolically 'cooks' the raw material you work with, transforming the client's lead dross into the alchemist's gold. In order to discover the psyche's gold that is often hidden in dark places, the client must feel safe, protected and respected. It is your job to make sure this is always the case. Please be ethically and morally impeccable in all your interactions.

Some state and federal jurisdictions require all business professionals in any field who collect personal information from clients to post the Privacy Policy for their organization so that clients will be able to determine if their personal information will remain private. Check your government services office and any applicable licensing boards to ensure that you are in compliance and not accidentally breaking any privacy laws.

In summary, both parties ought to expect (and demand) confidentiality, honesty, ethical dealings and mutual respect between each other during the work. Always seek permission and never make assumptions about what is acceptable to the client, otherwise one can cause even more trauma. When in doubt, ask! The initial client intake process is very important for clarifying the client's needs, situation, and setting the proper intention for the soul retrieval work. Remember:

- Keep privacy and confidentiality utmost in mind;

## Section Two – Preparation and Paperwork

- People need to feel safe. Work on establishing trust with your client – it is an essential element for the success of the process. In order to receive the healing they must have trust and faith in the practitioner;
- Actively listen to the client so they feel they are heard and respected;
- Always search for ways to engage the client in their personal healing process and have them own all parts of the healing;
- Tell the client to bring a journal so they can record important material. People are encouraged to be in the moment and experience the soul retrieval rather than be in their head while it is happening. However, that often means they may forget some of the details afterwards unless they are written down;
- Encourage the client to bring a witness (or their whole family if they wish) who can support them and be their 'designated driver' to get them home afterwards. It is much nicer for the client if they do not immediately have to cope with driving and dealing with ordinary reality directly after the soul retrieval;
- **Always** maintain personal and professional boundaries with clients. This specifically and emphatically means *absolutely no sexual contact*;
- Don't validate or invalidate someone's sexual abuse beliefs;
- 90% of the work is preparation and setting the proper intention with the client; 10% of the work is doing the actual soul retrieval journey;
- Be impeccable in all your words and actions. Do not say words or make promises to the client that you do not mean or cannot follow through on later;

- 'No.' is a complete sentence. You are the professional in charge of the service being offered to a client. Do not feel obligated or pressured into doing anything you are not comfortable with – you do not have to explain or justify your refusal to do something;
- When in doubt, ask Spirit.

## *Setting up Sacred Space*

While each practitioner will bring their own values, strengths and emphasis to their practice, all core shamanism courses follow a similar path of learning, including journeying, retrieving power animals, spiritual healing, soul retrieval, etc. All of these practices require the agency of 'spirit.' What the term spirit means here is all of the material and immaterial forms of conscious energy that surround us.

Spirit empowers us, lifts us up, and is the real 'muscle' that accomplishes our sacred work. To aid us in our shamanic practice we personify spirit and often name it, such as 'the Helping Spirits.' In order to perform shamanic activities, we must invite the Helping Spirits to assist us inside sacred space. You can also acknowledge the ancestors, the elements, the spirit of the land and the nature spirits who lovingly provide their help. Sacred space is created to surround the physical space we work in. It separates you and your client from any non-beneficial energy that may be in your proximity while doing energy healing work. Sacred space helps to focus our intention and resonates with the vibration of a space where we have meditated and raised the energy of our surroundings through past intentions. It is our own 'private universe' where we use our feelings, intention, energy and prayer to lovingly work in union with spirit.

Sacred space is a container holding the intention of love and healing for the client, even before they physically step into the space and the Helping Spirits are invoked to do the work. It is not as much a process used to do healing work, but the emotion and intention used in creating and holding sacred space that provides the best 'catalyst' and most salubrious atmosphere where healing can occur.

It is a good idea to have a fixed physical location set aside to use for your sacred work, and to always use this particular space when meditating, journeying, and performing spiritual practice. The physical space we use becomes 'conditioned' over time; that is, it becomes more powerful as it is filled with energy that vibrates at a level in concordance with our healing intentions and positive thoughts. Recently, physicists experientially verified how and why this intentional conditioning happens. (For details on these interesting new discoveries, please see the reference to Tiller's *Conscious Acts of Creation: The Emergence of a New Physics* in the Sources and Further Readings section of this book.)

## *Becoming the Hollow Bone*

Anyone involved in energy healing work needs to be 'quiet.' By quiet, we mean in a state of centeredness, humility, joy, and feeling like 'the hollow bone.' Ego is minimized. We become aware of, and are one with, the flow of sacred energy throughout our body. We are living in this moment and not thinking about the past or worried about the future. We are detached from outcome.

Becoming the best 'hollow bone' possible involves four steps: quieting our body and our consciousness, tuning into and perceiving our own energy state, setting our conscious intention, and allowing spirit to flow through us unimpeded by ego's desires. But what is the best way to accomplish all this?

Quieting our body and our consciousness is an important first step because it helps us enter and work in non-ordinary reality. There are a number of ways to quiet our internal systems, both with physical and mental exercises. Traditional methods to accomplish this quieting process include yoga and other energetic exercises, prayer, breathwork, chanting, drumming, rattling, and meditation. Strive for a combination of both physical exercise and mental meditation in whatever form feels most pleasant and effective for your daily personal practice.

The quieter our internal systems are, the more we can perceive energy and work consciously with spirit. The need for quiet internal systems may seem like a bit of a paradox when we are beating a drum and loudly chanting or singing while journeying with the Helping Spirits!

## Section Two – Preparation and Paperwork

However, accepting paradox is the feminine perspective of seeing and living your life with heart, whereas seeing and accepting objects as being in opposition to each other has traditionally been the masculine means of perceiving the world around us. Accepting paradox is a unique gift that we learn when walking the path with heart, helping us to become more aware of the immense and silent power hidden within us.

Qigong is a wonderful means for quieting internal systems and gaining a clearer perception of subtle energy flows throughout the body, involving slow physical body movements and a cultivation of the perception and movement of life force (chi) energy. You can experience this through a local yoga studio course or refer to a Qigong training DVD for an introduction to this powerful form of exercise.

Once you have quieted the body's systems you will sense more of the subtle energy flows within yourself and others. The perception of energy states involves going within and turning our senses inwards. Traditionally this has involved a meditative practice such as shamanic journeying, prayer, walking in nature or listening to meditative chants, such as mantras. Placing your awareness in your heart chakra or the pituitary gland inside your head (through the use of conscious intention) is also a good way to 'go inward' to focus on the subtle energies. Being in your heart center can give you access to feelings and emotional states that can add to the total picture you are sensing. Focusing awareness in your pituitary gland provides an easier connection to higher consciousness, while at the same time staying in your body and remaining aware of your own body's energy flows. Each person will have different strengths and preferences for how they sense subtle energy, so try them all – soft vision, feelings, intuition, sound, sensation, or just knowing – to find your best way in. Then trust what you sense.

Journey and ask Spirit for ways to become the hollow bone. Here is a mantra I use to help focus inward and empower my spiritual practice:

- Sit comfortably with straightened back, in your sacred space.
- Relax. Calm your mind and your body.
- Call in the message of the mantra you want to use: be mindful of its power and origination.
- Say "Thank you, thank you, thank you" to show appreciation and respect. The first "thank you" is to Spirit, the second is to your Helping Spirits, and the third is to your self – your body, mind and soul.
- Begin chanting your mantra either aloud or silently; either way will enhance the benefits desired.
- You can visualize light flowing through the body if this aids you.
- Empty the mind: don't think, just focus on the chant and visualization. Let your awareness remain in the heart or the pituitary center in the brain.
- Chant for as long as you are able, while maintaining a state of joyfulness.
- When you are done say "Thank you, thank you, thank you" to show appreciation and respect.

Section Two – Preparation and Paperwork

- Return the message of the mantra back to the spirits by saying: "The spirit of the mantra, and all other spirits here, please return to the spiritual world."

Here are some ways I have used to deepen and strengthen my spiritual practice:

- I quiet my systems, center inside to permit the flow of life force energy, allowing perception to unfold, *and only then* begin my work.
- I drink lots of water and stay hydrated. If I am dehydrated then my energy cannot flow through the body as easily, and I cannot perceive subtle energies as well.
- I use continuous deep breaths to stay centered and keep my energy flowing. If my energy is flowing and I am full of spirit, I will not take on any misplaced energies.
- Energy follows emotion and intention. I try to be impeccable in my thoughts and actions while at work – no distractions and maintaining positive thoughts at all times.
- I am careful what music I play in the background, as my body's energy system entrains with the music's vibration and resonates with it. (The result of this entrainment may or may not be what you desire.)

*"There is no 'out there' out there."*
— Alain Herriott

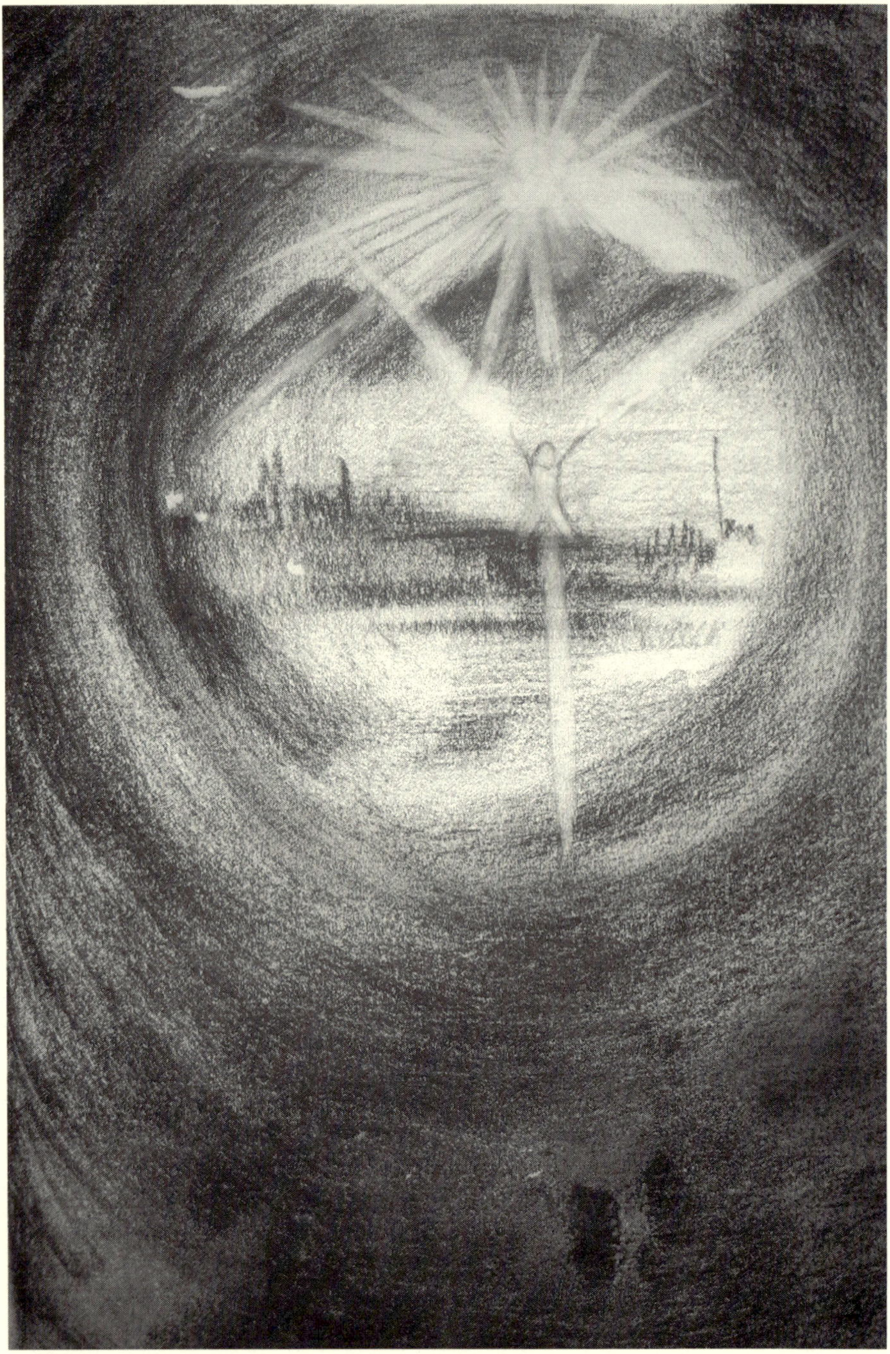

# Section Three – The Core Process

## *Love, not Technique*

Once all of the preliminary work is complete, the actual soul retrieval process is fairly straightforward: you have the proper intention, you are in sacred space, your client is prepared, and you can now journey to ask your power animals and Helping Spirits to assist you in tracking down and returning your client's lost soul essence. You can think of it as a similar process to retrieving a power animal for a client, with some additional steps and possible complications if the lost soul essence needs assistance to begin its return voyage. More than one piece of soul essence can be tracked down and retrieved during a single soul retrieval journey. However, a client must then be given sufficient time to assimilate what has been returned before having another soul retrieval. Generally speaking, a practitioner will retrieve no more than two or three pieces of soul essence at a time; it can take weeks or months for the client to integrate just one soul part or multiple pieces that are retrieved during a journey.

What is described here is a general process that is a good starting point. However, be aware that this is only a basic template. Your Helping Spirits will guide the way and teach you as you gain more experience and evolve your own unique process. Everyone works with different strengths and perceptive qualities. For example, a female shaman may feel that SR work is a 'birth process' for soul essence to enter this world, whereas a male shaman may think of soul retrieval work as a 'fix-it repair' of what has broken down. In any case, the most important thing to remember is that your love and compassion in harmony with Spirit helps the healing to occur, more so than techniques used to do the work.

Normally these 'undocumented lessons' are verbally transmitted in ceremony to shamanic students at the right time, when they are prepared and such work is appropriate. You would not be preparing to learn soul retrieval unless the Helping Spirits already knew you were ready to do this important work. So now let us begin!

## *Initial Practitioner Preparation*

In your own process of initially learning how to perform soul retrieval, you need to first journey and determine what particular power animal or teacher will work with you when you are performing this work.

You may find there is more than one helper who wishes to assist you. Welcome them all into your healing practice, and thank them with your love and gratitude for their offer of help and guidance.

You will also journey and ask for 'a metaphor of receiving' that you can use to welcome your own soul parts back home. This may be an image of a sponge soaking up water, doors opening wide to receive you, a house with its windows open to receive the breeze, or a flower opening to the rays of the sun. When working with clients, they will journey and find their own metaphor of receiving before you do the actual SR with them, and you will use their metaphor when working on their behalf. Also, both you and the client must drink lots of water in preparation for the work so your energy systems are flowing smoothly. Dehydration inhibits energy from flowing.

## *Client Preparation for the Journey*

The first thing that needs to be done is ensuring that the client knows how to journey. In soul retrieval work you want to 'give them a job' and skillfully engage their assistance. They need to be in a receptive state and empowered to help in their own healing. If the client does not know how to journey, you can still do the soul retrieval. However, the effect may not be as profound for them, and the healing may not last, if they have not invested their own energy in the work. The work can still have a deep effect, however a viable connection with spirit will help them integrate their soul essence and continue to heal. Thus, to better ensure success in the work, they need to know how to journey. If the client does not feel there is an urgent need for SR you can encourage them to learn how to journey first and actively start them on the shamanic path. An overview for teaching a client to journey is outlined in the Annex.

The intention for the client on this initial journey is to "journey with the intention of finding a 'metaphor of receiving' for your soul retrieval." Give them some examples and tell them that the metaphor helps to welcome and integrate the soul essence when it returns. If a client is unable or unwilling to journey, they can simply rest in a state of openness and give you permission to journey on their behalf.

Perform the journey with the client, so that they are supported in this work, and then give them time to absorb the information they receive. Your journey alongside them provides protection and sacred space for them to safely explore non-ordinary reality for a brief time. You may also be given additional information that is needed for doing the soul retrieval work with this client.

Before teaching anyone how to journey, it is important to ensure they are clearly able to distinguish ordinary reality from NOR. People with disorders such as schizophrenia are unable to clearly distinguish between ordinary and non-ordinary reality. In such circumstances, it is better for you to journey on their behalf and determine the specific details for the healing.

Section Three – The Core Process

## *Making Room*

You can either have an assistant drum or play a drumming CD to provide the beat for journeying. Having an assistant is always preferable since they can also help hold sacred space, be a witness to the work, and record anything that needs to be written down. Have your rattle and any other power objects you feel will be useful, at hand. Your preparatory journeys to the Helping Spirits may have also revealed additional information or objects that would be useful for working with this client. All should be accessible within your sacred space. Smudge yourself and your client with sage. The client will lie down on a comfortable mat that you have already prepared. Ensure they are relaxed and comfortable, with a pillow and blanket in case they feel cool or desire the security of being covered. Ask the client for permission to physically touch them during the work when necessary, and be prepared to modify your technique in an appropriate manner if they prefer not to be touched.

You may or may not need to do some energy extraction work before the soul retrieval – the client may have some energy that does not belong to them, or they may need to 'make room' for the returning soul essence if this was indicated by the Helping Spirits in your preparations. If so, ask the client for their permission to do the extraction work that will assist them in receiving the soul part upon its return.

Energy extraction work can be potentially dangerous for the practitioner. It should only be done when you are completely filled with spirit and have merged with the personal Helping Spirit you use for healing work. Rather than giving a detailed set of instructions in this book, a summary of some points to remember are provided in the Annex at the end of the document. However, please refer to your own course notes on energy extraction, review the process, and be clear on how it is correctly done before you begin.

## *The Soul Retrieval Journey*

You can take a short break after completing any energy extraction work, giving both the client and yourself a moment to rest and center. Clearly explain what you are going to do next, and what you want the client to do during the soul retrieval journey. The client needs to be open and willing to receive the returning essence. Ask the client to visualize their 'metaphor of receiving,' that you both will use to welcome their soul parts back home. You will use their metaphor of receiving when you are returning the soul essence back into their being. Ask the client to imagine this image while you are blowing the soul part into them.

Tell the client that it is traditional for the practitioner to lie on the floor next to the client, touching at shoulders, hips, and ankles, while retrieving the lost soul essence for them. Get the client's permission to do this and do not just assume that they will feel comfortable doing this. Remember: touching the client or lying beside them may cause additional trauma. If they are not comfortable with this posture, you can simply sit on the floor next to them during the journey.

Section Three – The Core Process

## *Tracking the Soul Essence*

When you are ready to begin the soul retrieval, open sacred space and begin drumming. The practitioner will normally be lying down beside the client or sitting next to them, as appropriate.

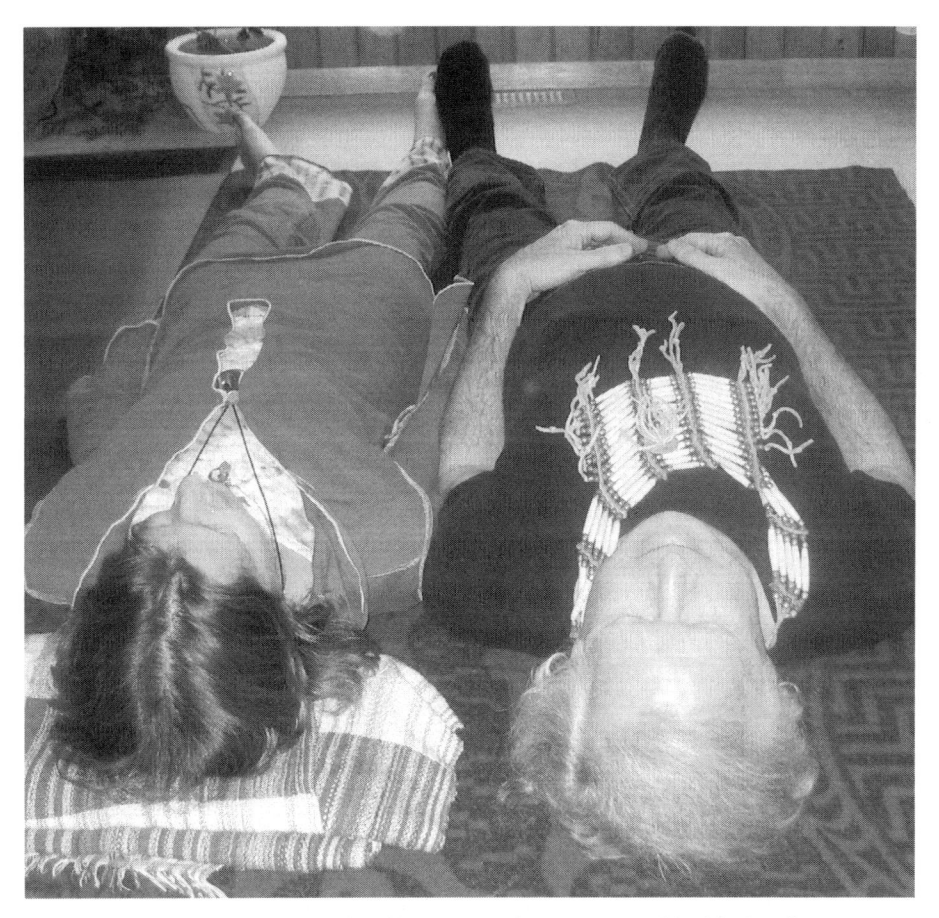

Figure 1. Beginning the soul retrieval journey to the Lower World with the client.

You will journey with the intention that has been worked out and agreed to in the dialogue between you and the client. This intention will normally be something like: "I am journeying to ask my Helping Spirits for their assistance in retrieving lost soul parts that wish to return to _____ (client's name) at this time."

Journey to the Lower World using the normal route and actions you take to enter Non-Ordinary Reality. Meet with your power animal or the Helping Spirit previously identified as the entity or entities that will assist you in the soul retrieval work. Ask for their help in finding the lost soul parts of the client you are journeying with. Follow them to where they take you. They are there to guide and protect you during this journey and will help lead you to the soul essence you are searching for. When you are tracking a client in NOR, you can use either their clothing or jewelry as a means of identifying the soul essence. The 'person' you meet may look like a recognizably younger version of the client, but this is not necessarily the case. It could, for example, turn out to be the *in situ* fetus of your client. Your intuition will also help you identify the lost soul part. Once you have this identified, you can begin the retrieval process.

## *Retrieving the Soul Essence*

At this time in their life, your client may not be consciously aware of the soul part(s) you have found and the associated trauma, so it is useful to first gather some intelligence about the situation and what the soul part represents. Tell the soul part who you are and why you are seeking the lost soul part on behalf of the client.

The essence you meet will most likely resemble a younger version of the client or else represent a metaphor of the original trauma. For example, you might find a small child chained to a table in the basement. This does not necessarily mean that the original real life trauma involved your client being chained in the basement; the chains will most likely be a metaphor for how the soul essence interpreted or felt about the situation it thought occurred. Think of this metaphor as a dream, observing the symbols of this drama just like you would observe one of your own dreams. Later, when you awake, you have the opportunity to interpret the significance of the actors, actions, objects and feelings experienced in the dream. In the soul retrieval journey, ask the soul part:

Who are you?

When did you leave?

Why did you leave? Why did you have to go?

What was your pain? Who hurt you? Why did you feel hurt?

Tell me about your gifts, wisdom, medicine, beauty and talents that you possess.

How can my client honor you now?

How will the client grow if you return to them?

What changes does the client need to make in their life to accommodate you?

What old parts of the client must die for you to live within them?

**Most important**: would you like to return home to your Soul?

## The Essence of Soul Retrieval

Let the soul part know that the situation that originally caused the trauma has now ended. Tell the essence what has changed in the client's life and how the client will welcome it back as a desired part of their being. Ask the soul part to come back with you if it feels right.

The soul essence may not be ready to return immediately, or may be unable to return without your assistance. The soul essence may want to return a week (or several months) later when the client has properly prepared for its return. You can offer truthful reassurances and new information that the soul part does not know about the client's life since it left, however do not trick or force the soul part to return with you. If the timing is not right, the soul retrieval work may be postponed until a later time. It is also possible that other lost soul parts are ready and able to return with you. You can ask your power animal and Spirit Helper to track down these other lost soul parts and follow their lead.

There are circumstances where a soul part cannot return because it was taken by (or given to) someone else. In these cases you need to follow the luminous cord connecting the soul part to the energetic representation of the person who has the client's energy. Use your power animals and Spirit Helpers to track the connection to its source. Traditionally, the shaman would use some form of trickery to get the soul thief to release the essence it was holding. However, our objective here is to do no harm; there are more compassionate ways to release the soul part. Dialogue with the soul thief and find out why it has the soul part. The thief may want what the soul part represents, may be burdened by its presence, or not even aware that it is holding onto this energy. Ask your Helping Spirits and power animal for assistance in providing what the thief needs. We can never use the energy of another soul, however we can feel burdened by holding onto such energy. If you can provide something the thief needs in exchange for the soul part, then the work can be done in a respectful form of reciprocity. Once you have gained the release of the lost soul part, you can break the luminous cord connecting the soul essence to the thief and return that soul part to the client.

It is also possible to experience a client's soul part as being 'impacted' within them, rather than having been split off and lost. It may appear to have retreated deep within. We cannot retrieve what has not left; in this case soul retrieval will not work. Instead we can help this soul part to reemerge. Both you and the client can journey to find an appropriate ritual that will allow this healing to occur.

Power animals can represent the instinctual parts of the self. Often a new power animal will reveal itself and want to return along with the lost soul part that has been retrieved for the owner. When this happens you can gather up the power animal and return it to the client in the same manner you normally use for power animal retrievals.

When you are ready to return the essence(s) to the client, bring your arms up and hold your arms outstretched. Tell the soul part (and power animal) to come back with you. Focus your intention and concentrate on feeling their energy come to you. Slowly and gently pull the energy down into your heart with all your concentration. Welcome them into your embrace with love and compassion. This moment is often a joyous experience of ecstasy for the shamanic practitioner connecting the soul essence with the practitioner's heart.

# The Essence of Soul Retrieval

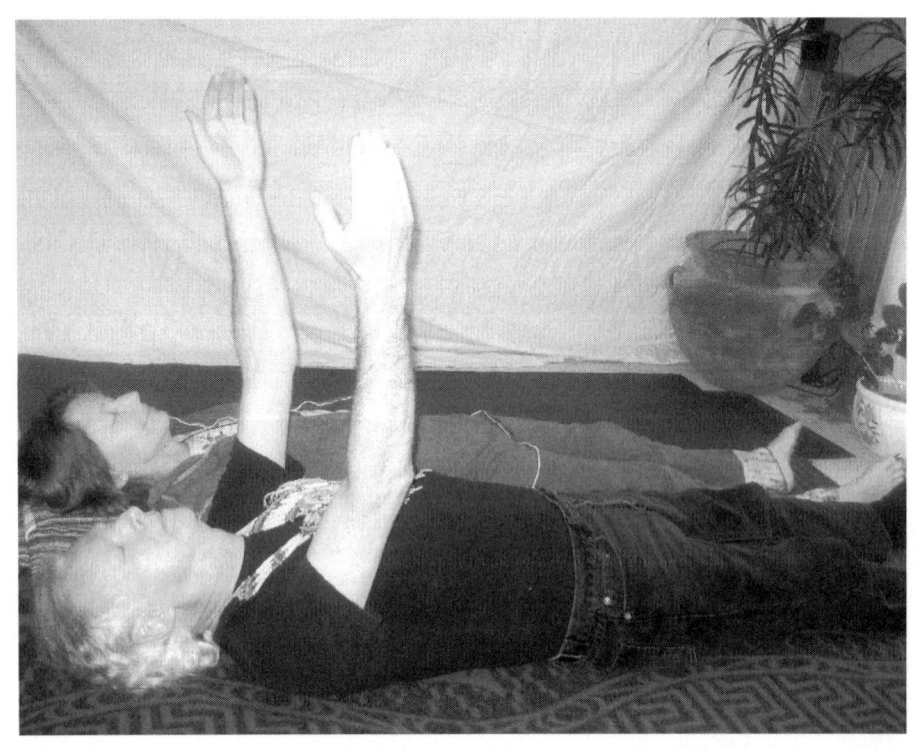

Figure 2. Stretch out your arms with love and receive the lost soul part when it is ready to return with you.

Section Three – The Core Process

Figure 3. Pull the soul essence into your heart. You can also attach it to a necklace or power object that you use to protect and carry soul energy during the SR journey.

Ensure that all of the essence, including returning soul parts and power animals, is pulled into your heart or tightly attached to your necklace or other personal power object intended to protect and carry soul parts during your journey. (This could be a crystal, shamanic mirror, pi stone or other sacred object that you have charged with the intention of carrying out this work.)

## *Returning and Restoring the Soul Essence*

Drawing your arms down to your chest is the signal your drummer has been watching for. They can gently end the drumming and begin the callback signal to assist you and your client in journeying back to ordinary reality. If possible, ask for a longer than normal callback drum beat until the drummer observes you are conscious, since it can take longer to return to ordinary reality in this type of journey. If you are listening to a drumming CD, you can still make your return from Non-Ordinary Reality and follow the steady drumbeat back home.

Follow your power animal or Helping Spirit in NOR and make your way back to the place where you entered their reality. Thank them for their help in locating the lost soul essence and for allowing you to enter their realm to do this work. You can lie down in an underground river and symbolically cleanse yourself to wash away any energy that does not belong in our world and must not return with you. (This is an especially useful action if you are empathic and feel the pain of the client during shamanic work.) You can also use some other cleansing ritual that your own Helping Spirits have given to you. Then follow the drumbeat of your callback signal and return to your body in ordinary reality.

Section Three – The Core Process

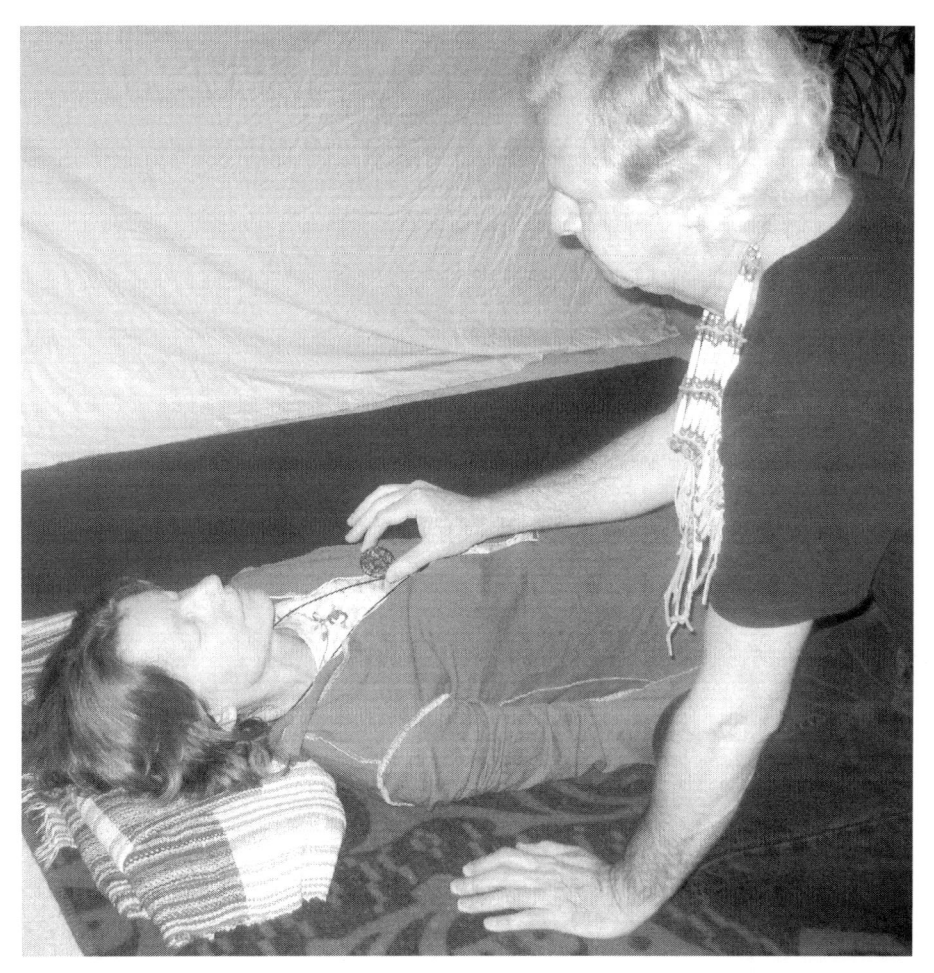

Figure 4: Position yourself next to your client, take the power object (a pi stone in this example) and cup your hands over the heart.

Sit up and position yourself alongside your client so you can return the soul essence to them. Focus your attention on the soul part that is held either in your heart or protected in the power object you used to carry the soul part. Cup your hands together, and with intense feeling and intention blow the soul essence into their heart. Imagine the soul energy leaving your heart or sacred object, traveling out of your hands and into

## The Essence of Soul Retrieval

the client's heart. Do this with great concentration – use all of your senses to feel, taste, touch, smell and see the essence go into the client's heart.

Feel this energy flowing into and through their whole body with love and compassion. Imagine this new energy infusing every cell of their body and awakening a renewed sense of wellbeing and health within them. Envisage the client receiving this returned soul energy with the 'metaphor of receiving' they have chosen.

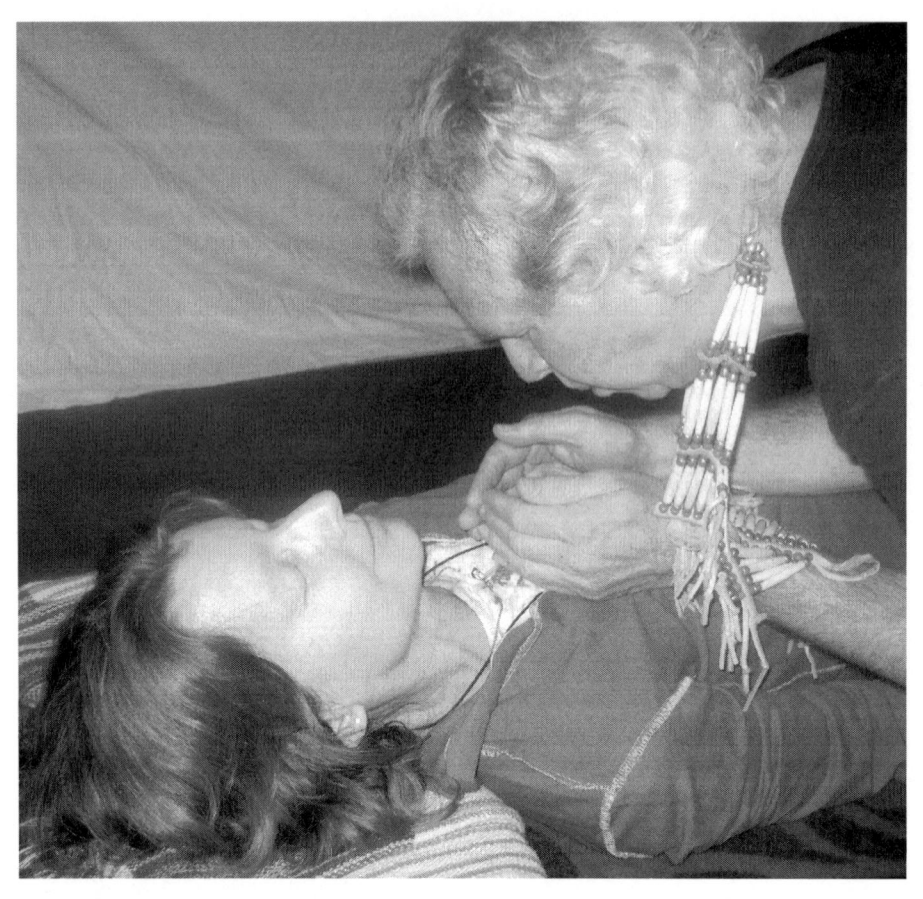

Figure 5. With cupped hands, blow the soul essence into your client's heart while invoking the 'metaphor of receiving' that the client has chosen.

## Section Three – The Core Process

If a power animal has also returned for the client, this energy will also be blown into the client's heart and crown at the same time as the soul essence is restored. Imagine the energy of the power animal filling the space around every cell in their body.

Once you have blown the energy through the heart, move to the head and repeat the previous step, blowing the soul energy into the crown and down through the whole body.

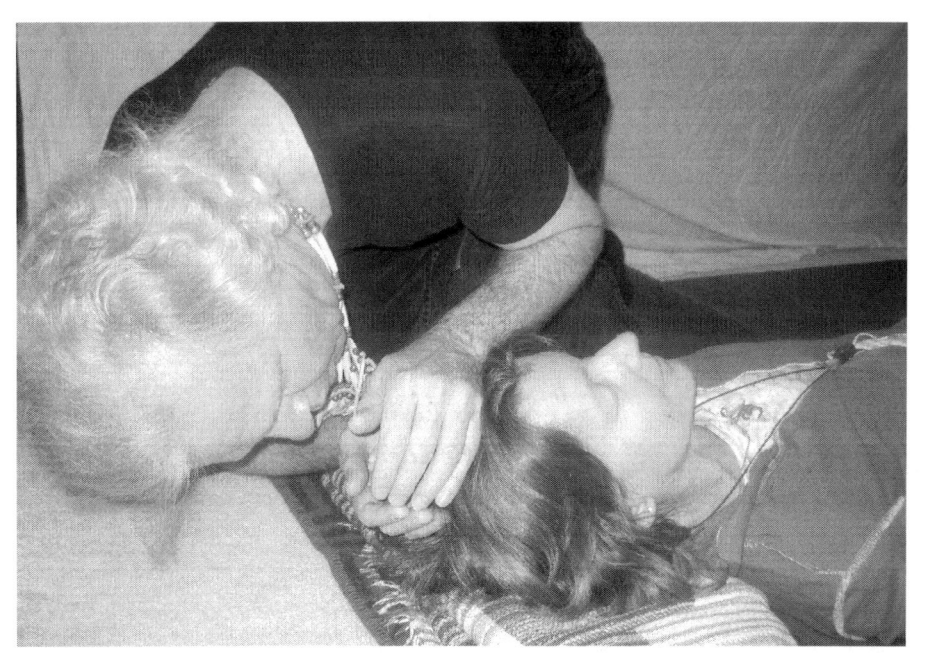

Figure 6. Blow the soul essence into your client's crown using the same intention as was used for the heart.

The Essence of Soul Retrieval

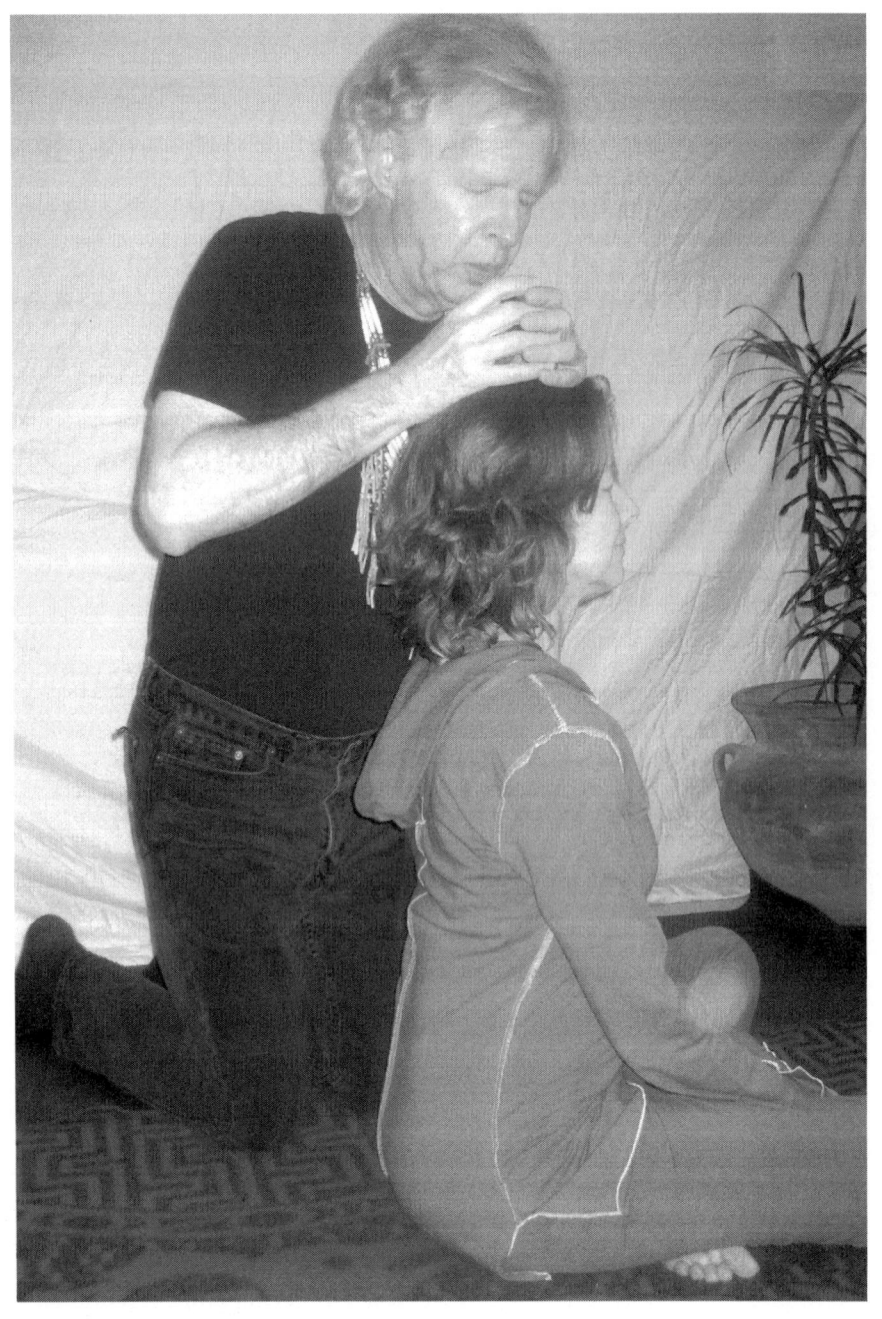

Figure 7. Alternatively, you can have the client sit up while you blow the soul essence into their crown and through the body.

## Section Three – The Core Process

Once you feel that your client has received the soul essence and the instinctual energy of the power animal, seal the vital energy into the spirit body of the client. Use a rattle to seal both the heart and crown entry points, the same as you would at the site of any energy extraction work. Visualize these areas being sealed like the closing of a door. Rattle around the entire body four times to seal it. (Journey to your Helping Spirits to find your own personal way of sealing off the spirit body.)

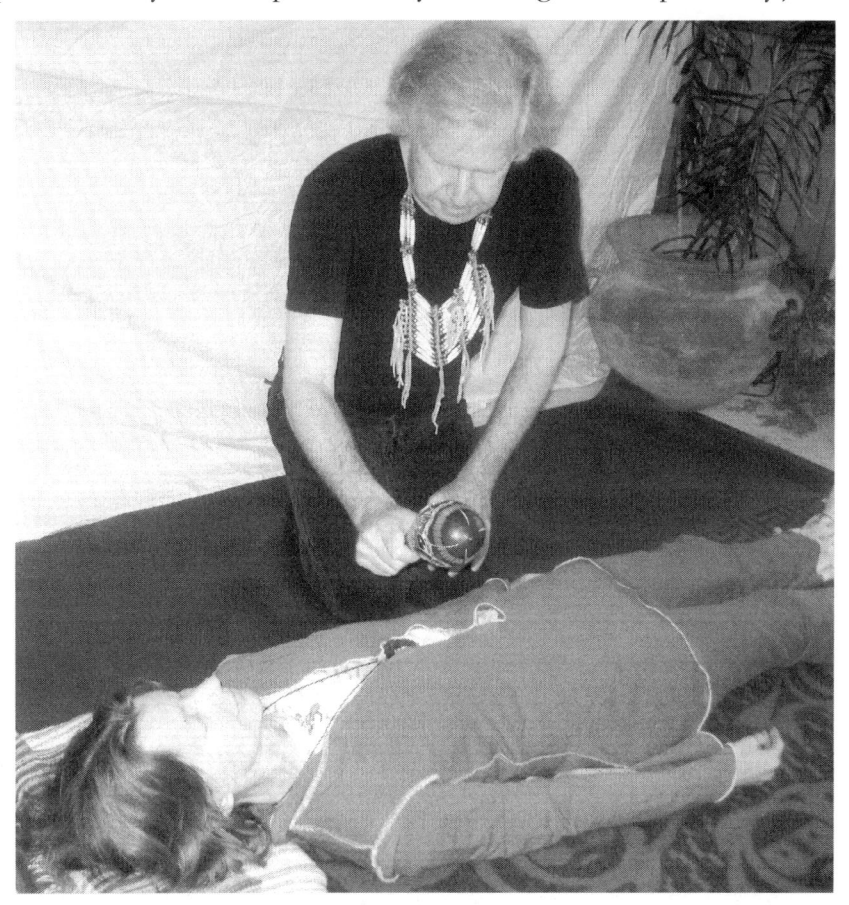

Figure 8. Seal the soul essence into your client's **heart** using your rattle, and visualize the area being sealed like the closing of a door.

# The Essence of Soul Retrieval

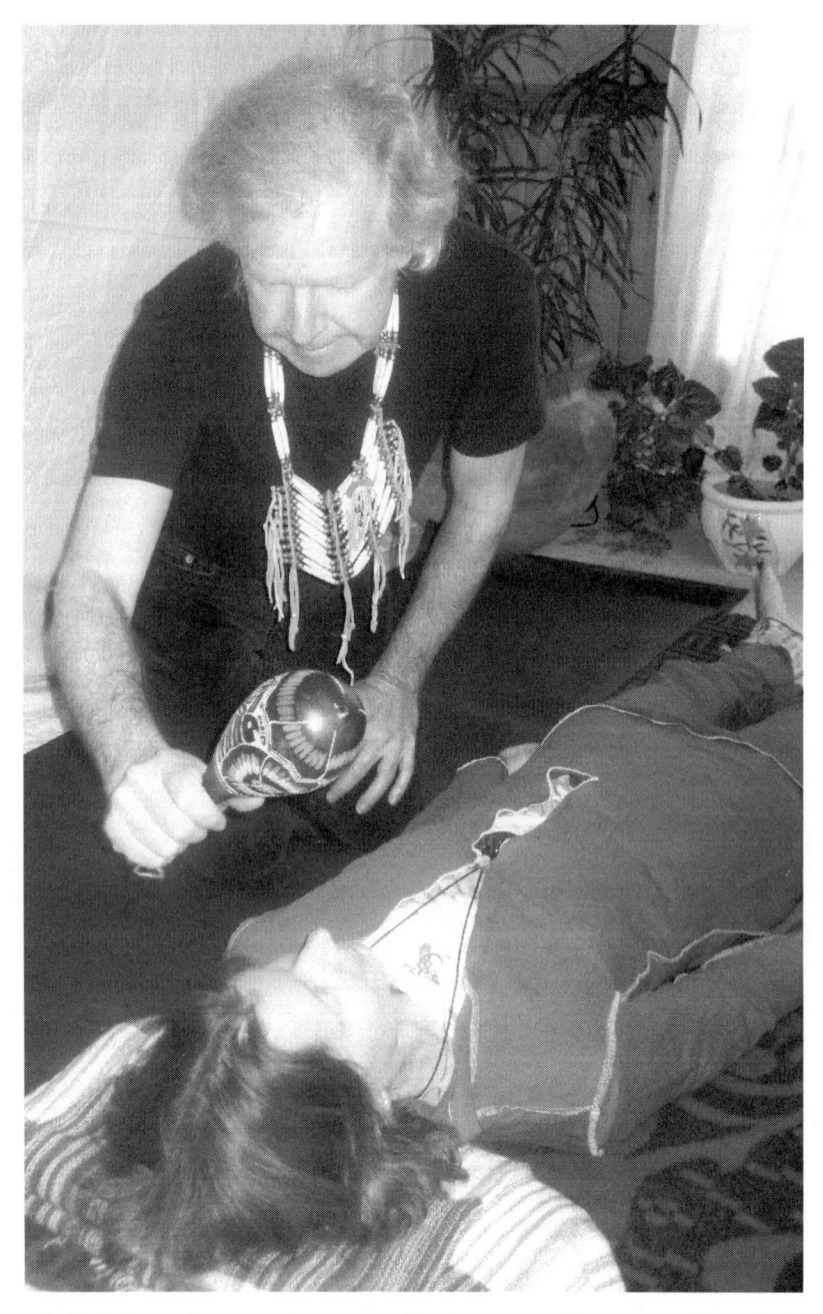

Figure 9. Seal the soul essence into your client's **crown** using your rattle, and visualize the area being sealed like the closing of a door.

Section Three – The Core Process

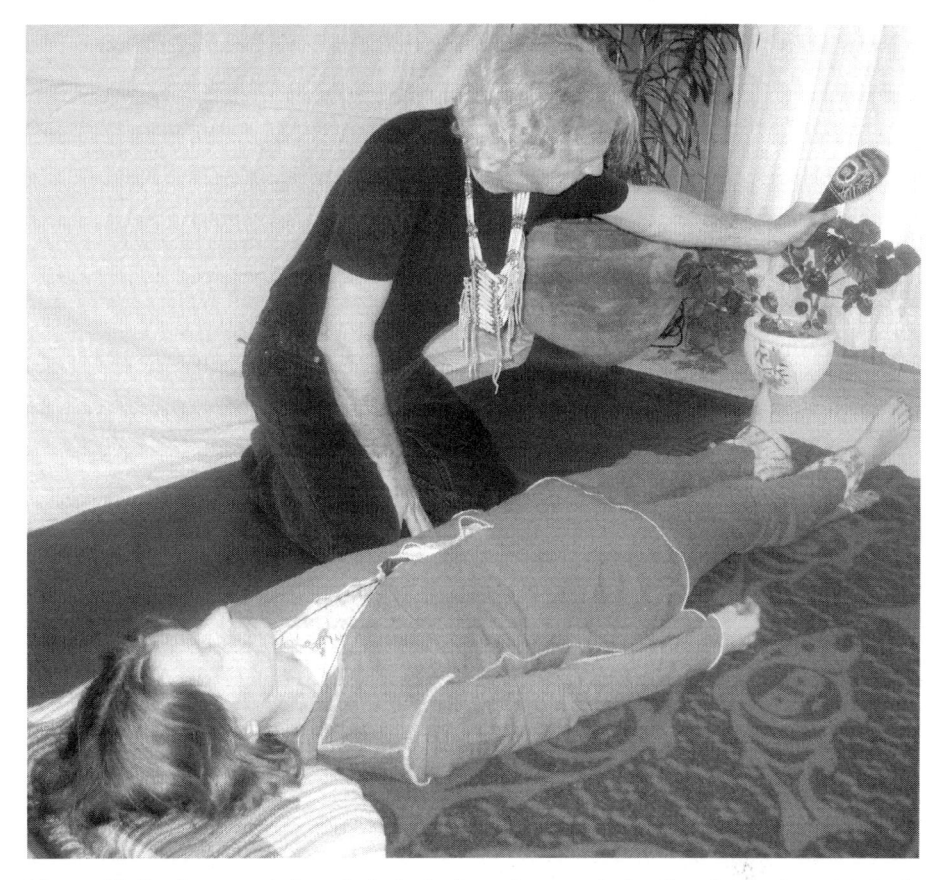

Figure 10. Rattle around the whole body four times and visualize the entire spirit body being sealed like the closing of a door.

## *Completing the work*

Your soul retrieval journey is complete! The rattling sound will have helped your client return to ordinary reality. You can lightly touch them on their shoulder to assist them in feeling at home in their body. Holding their feet can also help them ground the experience. When they

## The Essence of Soul Retrieval

appear conscious, peer into your client's eyes and welcome home the returned soul essence with joy and love in your heart. "Welcome home!"

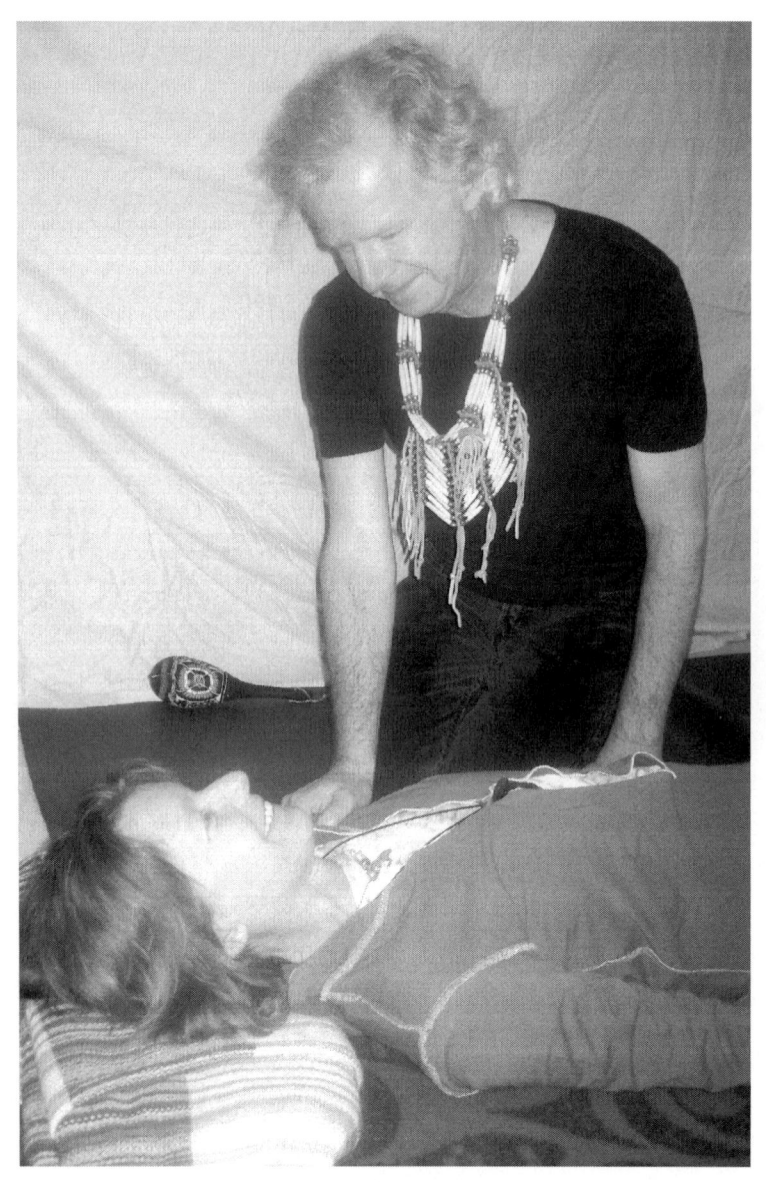

Figure 11. Peer into your client's eyes and welcome home the returned soul essence with joy and love in your heart.

## Section Three – The Core Process

Allow the client as much time as they need to center and return to full consciousness. They may feel dizzy from their journey, or emotionally overwhelmed by this soul energy they are experiencing, possibly for the first time in many years. The client can have a variety of responses to the soul retrieval. They may cry, be elated, laugh, feel expanded; everyone reacts differently. Whatever response they have is an experience unique unto them. The returning soul essence may take some time to fully settle in their body. It is essential *not* to begin a conversation, and to leave the logical left side of the brain alone for the moment. What the client is *feeling* is essential for the integration of the soul part. The story is of lesser importance. The experience is the most important part, and you don't want to take them out of their heart and back to their head. As soon as possible, suggest they go out into nature for a short 10-minute walk to hug a tree or sit quietly and ground the experience. Ask them to invite the tree to help them anchor the newly returned soul essence into their being.

# The Essence of Soul Retrieval

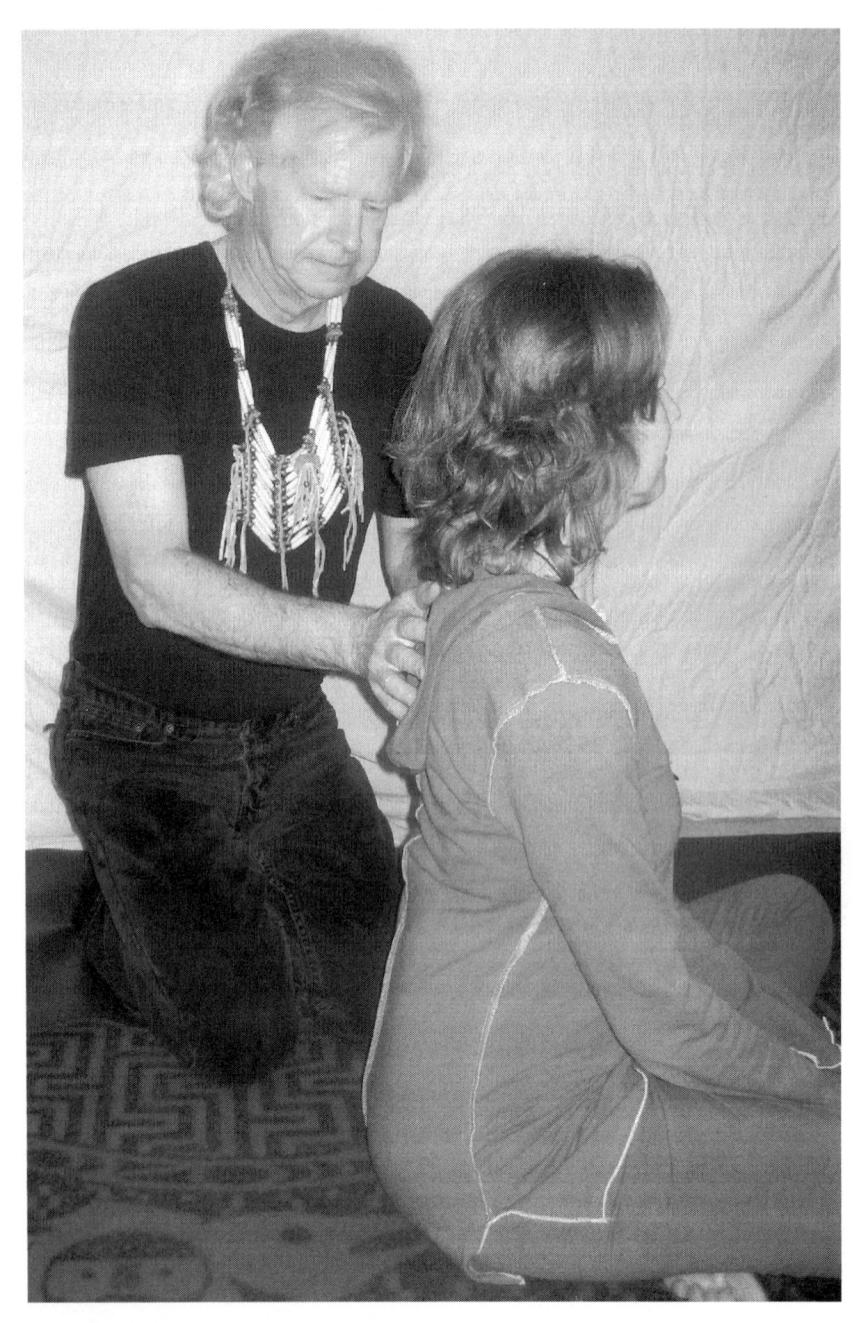

Figure 12. Allow your client time to return to ordinary reality, and then suggest they go out into nature for a brief time in order to ground the experience.

While the client is taking some time attending to their self to ground the experience, you have the opportunity to write down any important notes about the journey so they are not forgotten later. (This time may also be used productively to journey for a healing story.)

## *Journeying for a Healing Story*

Retrieving the lost soul part is often a journey of ecstasy, quickly accomplished with the guidance of the Helping Spirits. However, keeping the client and the newly returned soul essence 'intact' afterwards is also an important component. The 'healing story' and the continuing integration work given to the client assists in accomplishing this task.

Once the client has returned from their walk, ask how they are feeling and prepare them for the last journey of the day. If the client has been taught how to journey, they can also do 'an integration journey' alongside of you for their own benefit. One question/intention that the client can journey on with you is: "Journey to the soul essence that has returned and ask it to show you how you can bring more harmony and passion into your life's work. Ask it to show or tell you what commitment you need to make to your new soul part." Involving the client in this work empowers them and commits then to their own healing process. If they

## The Essence of Soul Retrieval

can't journey, invite them to imagine writing a letter of commitment or conversing with their newly returned soul part.

Your task now is to journey for a healing story to share with your client. Ask them to lie down once again beside you, and state your intention of receiving a healing story. Also state the intention of the client's integration journey so they understand what they need to do. Begin the drumming, journey to the lower world and receive whatever healing story unfolds for you in whatever form it is delivered. Normally this will be a quick ten-minute journey.

Section Three – The Core Process

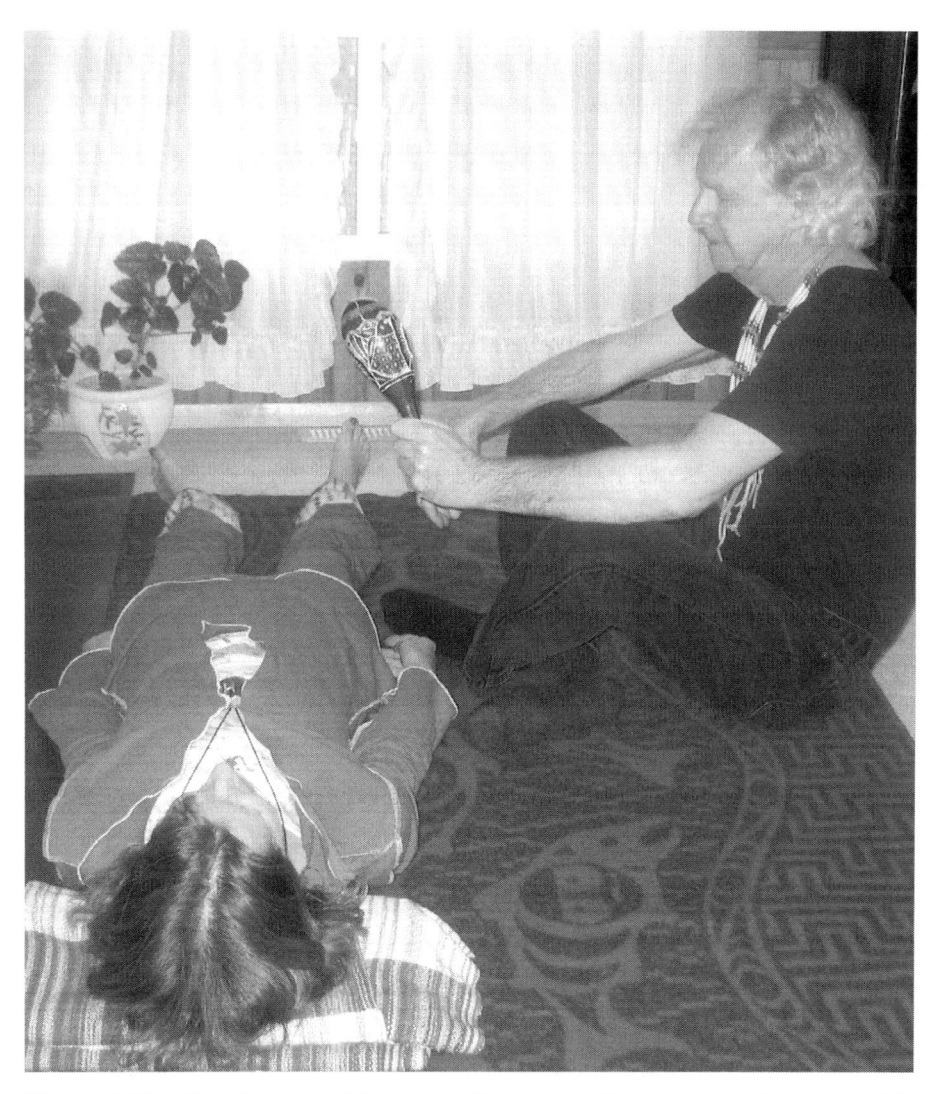

Figure 13. The client journeys with you to help integrate the returned soul essence, while you receive a healing story.

When you have completed your journey, you will often be able to intuitively sense that the client has completed their journey at almost the same moment. Signal for the callback drumming to begin, and return to ordinary reality. Again, allow the client time to return from non-ordinary

## The Essence of Soul Retrieval

reality and give them a few moments to make some notes if they wish. You can also write down the main points from the healing story.

## *Sharing the Soul Retrieval Journey*

Your client may be a bit shy or overwhelmed by what was experienced during the soul retrieval process, so you may offer to share your experience first. However, when you are sharing information about your soul retrieval journey, always be very mindful of the words you are using.

Although you are comfortable working in non-ordinary reality with power animals and spirit helpers, your client may not be open to such a metaphorical interpretation of reality and how consciousness operates in Non-Ordinary Reality. Your initial interactions provided you with some information on their background and belief systems. How open were they to the beliefs and concepts used in shamanism? Always try to ensure that all of your interactions give the client a feeling of respect and empowerment rather than a sense of anxiety raised by your use of peculiar language or beliefs. Reframe your words to make them more acceptable, avoiding areas that may conflict with their religious beliefs. A number of people have noted that when they hear the word 'shamanism' they unconsciously hear 'Satanism,' even though they know the speaker is talking about something totally different. Childhood experiences and culturally ingrained beliefs can often be a barrier to hearing and understanding new concepts. Many people, even while actively pursuing complementary and alternative forms of healing, will find energy healing practices such as shamanism, Reiki, and energy healing to be 'too far out there' to logically accept. Maintain a calm sense of compassion and love for everyone who is seeking healing, regardless of their beliefs.

Never pity or judge a client. Instead, imagine them in their divine light. Whenever we judge someone we send out an energy that makes them unconsciously want to hide their illness (or whatever they are emotionally concerned about) from us. This makes our job more challenging, so please act with compassion and from the heart at all times.

The next issue to consider when telling your SR story to the client concerns the content of the journey itself. Will what I say cause shock? The intention here is not to push the client back into a remembrance of the trauma that originally caused the soul loss. That is not the point of this work. However it can happen – even lying down next to them may trigger memories. You may see the original traumatic event during your journey. However, you only want to relate a positive experience to the client about the wonderful characteristics imbued by the returned soul essence. For this reason, be very careful what is said about your experience during the soul retrieval. You would not describe the visible characteristics of an energy entity removed during an extraction process; in a similar manner you must carefully edit your journey experience, removing any description of the original trauma.

Sandra Ingerman notes a skillful way to share the soul retrieval with the client. Rather than saying "I brought back a five-year old part of yourself," it is better to say "I brought back *the essence* that you lost when you suffered a trauma at the age of five." Your client will better understand that their pure life force was returned to them, and not a traumatized part, if this perspective is used when sharing your journey.

Give a general description of your journey to the client so that they know what your shamanic experience was like while retrieving their soul essence. Emphasize the positive characteristics that you learned about the soul parts (and power animal) that have been retrieved. (You may wish to consult Ted Andrews' Animal Speak book to determine the symbolic meaning and energetic force represented by power animals you retrieve.) When sharing a journey it is *critically important* that you tell the client you do not know if this journey can be interpreted in a metaphorical sense, like the symbols one sees in a dream or if it is to be interpreted in a literal way. The client must understand this distinction, otherwise they may fail to relate to the information and reject it because they can't make sense of it. In turn, you will begin to question your own competency and ability to do the work. Do not try to 'translate' symbols for the client either; seeing a turtle in your journey will not have the same symbolic meaning as the client seeing a turtle in their journey. It is up to the client to make sense of symbols and metaphors from the journey and to determine how it all fits into their life.

Give the client time to absorb the soul retrieval journey and ask if they have any questions you need to clarify. Ask if they feel comfortable sharing about their own journey and what they may have been asked to do to help assist in the integration of this soul essence. Be a good listener; do not attempt to 'reinterpret' or draw conclusions from the client's journey. It is their journey and, as in dream analysis, their symbols can have a totally different meaning than the same symbols do for your own unconscious psyche.

Finally, relate the healing story to the client using a calm and reassuring tone of voice.

## *What is a 'Healing Story?'*

The healing story for which you journey will often take the form of an allegory or fairytale-like story. It is simple, engaging both senses and feelings, and is direct in its personal meaning for the client. Tell the story in a voice that itself embodies a healing quality. This is an example of a healing story recounted to me by Martha Lucier from one of my own soul retrievals:

"There once was a very large tortoise. It was the oldest tortoise on earth. It was very special because it had no eyes to see, and no ears to hear. It also could not taste, or smell. The only sense that this tortoise had was intuition. Many times the tortoise would be swimming right beside sharks, but it was never harmed. It even swam into the mouth of a whale once, and found its way out using its intuition. This tortoise lived for over a thousand years because it trusted its intuition. It had to trust its intuition 100% and it grew so old because its intuition led the way to truth and love, and intuition didn't allow fear to stop the tortoise from living in the moment."

## *Theft of Soul Essence From Others*

During your soul retrieval work you may encounter a situation where someone has stolen the soul essence of another person. Possibly yourself, a client, or some other person that you meet in NOR has accidentally or intentionally taken or been given the soul essence of another person. For example, you may have given a part of your soul essence to a loved one, or a person may have selfishly taken the soul essence of another after traumatizing them. It is possible they may not even be aware that they have taken or been given the soul part. We cannot consciously use the energy taken from another soul, however we can feel burdened by holding onto that soul energy.

You can help by freeing the stolen soul energy from the person who has it. However, in this particular circumstance the rightful owner of the soul essence has not given us permission to retrieve the soul essence and return it back to them. Therefore, the essence must be returned to Spirit, and *not* to the person to whom it belongs. The owner may not be willing or able to receive it back, and it can cause difficulties for them if it is unexpectedly returned when they are not properly prepared. Giving the soul part to Spirit for safekeeping resolves this dilemma.

Section Three – The Core Process

## *Martha's Soul Retrieval Reminders for Learners*

Martha Lucier has a summary of reminders for soul retrieval:
- **Always** obtain client permission before doing any soul retrieval journeys.
- The client ought to refrain from using alcohol the day before and after SR, but they must continue on their regular medication schedule.
- Book at least two or three hours for the session.
- As a professional courtesy for the comfort of female clients, male practitioners are advised to consider bringing a female assistant.
- Always ask for permission to touch the client before doing any work.
- When tracking a client, use their clothing or jewelry as identification.
- Pay close attention to the seeds you are planting, with your words, when sharing afterwards.
- When sharing journeys, explain that you do not know if this is to be interpreted in a literal or metaphorical manner.
- You are returning pure soul essence to the client, not the traumatized part of their past experience.
- Do not pity the client; see them in their divine light.
- If you can't connect with your teacher/power animal then tell the client "today is not a good day to work."
- Ask the client to call you in 14 days to tell you how they are doing.
- Don't share if there is more essence that needs to return. Say that you'd like to set another appointment, as there is more work to do.

## The Essence of Soul Retrieval

- If you feel drained after the work, **you** are doing the work, not Spirit.
- Soul Stealing: Do no harm - ask your teacher/power animal for assistance in providing what the thief needs.
- No one can steal our soul if we do not let them. To prevent personal soul loss/stealing, fill yourself up with power of the divine.
- We can never use the energy of another soul, however we can feel burdened by holding onto it.

## *Other Tips for Learners to Remember*

- Work first with family/friends: "I've just learned a new energy healing method and I want to practice…"
- If working with a child, reframe your language and concepts to fit their worldview.
- It is your love and compassion that assists in healing, not technique!
- We do not heal anyone – the 'healer' is the person who is ill and wants to become well. We help facilitate the healing by working with Spirit.
- Our Spirit Helpers work on our behalf because of our honest and passionate intent. We are helping someone else to become fully alive and conscious in their being.
- Notice how your non-ordinary journey companions, your Spirit Helpers, always act in a compassionate manner. They are models of

## Section Three – The Core Process

compassionate action and behavior – pay attention and act in harmony with them.

- Notice the results of your work.
- Sometimes when we do the work, the universe provides what is most needed, not what is most desired.
- Make a connection with a therapist who can help if needed.
- Keep journeying and evolve your own work, as this is only the 'bare bones' overview of soul retrieval.
- You will develop your own unique style – Reiki, allopathic medical or psychotherapy practitioners – all add unique perspectives from their healing profession when they also do SR work.
- It is ok to have beginner's performance anxiety. Confidence will grow over time.

*"When you put a thing in order, and give it a name, and you are all in accord, it becomes."*
– from the Navajo, Frank Waters, *Masked Gods*

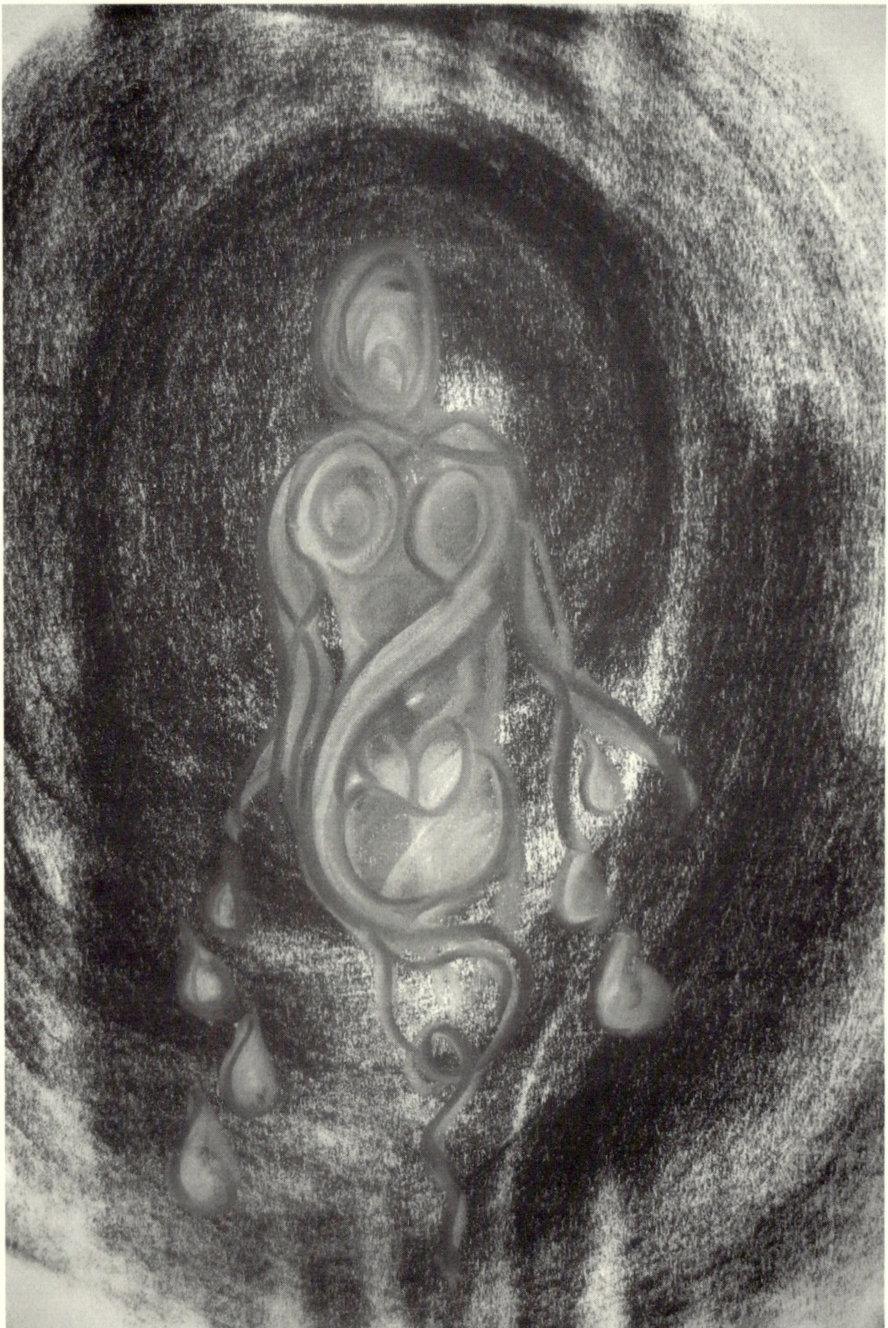

# Section Four – Client Support

## *Support and Follow-up*

Your task is now mostly done, while the client's work has just started. They need to continue the work of integrating the returned soul part into their full soul essence, and this takes time. It is necessary for them to begin forming a relationship with the returned soul essence. Here are some questions you can provide the client to think about, to journey on, and to ask the soul part:

> Tell me what are you here to help me accomplish in my life?
> What changes do I need to make in my life to accommodate you?
> What commitment do I need to make to my new soul part?

## The Essence of Soul Retrieval

Reassure the client that you are available via phone or email to assist them in this integration work, and that they will find it to be both inspiring and empowering to watch the process unfold over time. Let them know it is beneficial to journal their ongoing experience. Ask them to check in with you after two weeks to report how the work is unfolding. You can then answer any questions that might have arisen.

When you have completed your work, it is time to close sacred space, thank the Helping Spirits who lent their support and guidance for the soul retrieval work, and release them to go their own way. As closure to the ceremony, you and your client can go outside and offer some sacred tobacco as a thank you gift to the Helping Spirits.

It is also beneficial for the client to feel grounded before they leave. Walking in nature and reconnecting with the earth can help provide this anchoring. To ensure the client is fully back in their body and able to deal with ordinary reality, you can ask them some very concrete questions such as "What is the first thing you are going to do when you get home?"

If the client brought someone with them to assist them, it is beneficial to ask the support person to drive the client home so the client can have more time to stay in their heart and process the experience before having to deal with real world tasks such as driving a car. This is also the time to exchange gifts and receive payment in recognition of the time you have taken and work you have done together.

Section Four – Client Support

## *Client Recovery, Healing Crisis, Spiritual Bypass*

A soul retrieval can either produce 'fireworks' for the client or be a very subtle and long healing process as it unfolds. You may have been asked to address a particular issue for the client and then discover a totally different problem has been healed. It is interesting that the universe may give us what we most need, and not what we initially thought we really desired! Hopefully your client will leave with a clear understanding of what they need to do to integrate the life essence restored to them, but they may need additional help in the integration process. It is important to maintain contact with the client to ensure their relationship with this new soul essence is nurtured and honored so the client receives full benefit of the SR process.

Sandra Ingerman spends a lot time in her Soul Retrieval Newsletter emphasizing the importance of client follow-up. It can sometimes be difficult work. At the same time it can also be imperative for a client who does not fully understand the process or has a detrimental life habit interfering with the healing process. There may simply be more work to do with this particular client. For the practitioner, this should be recognized as an opportunity to do additional work with their clients. You are certainly justified in charging additional money for any follow-up work performed on their behalf. However, you must ensure there is clarity around what ongoing services are offered that will require payment.

When the effects of soul retrieval are very subtle, the client may not feel that they have a clear path to follow going forward, or may not feel motivated to seek out your help in a proactive manner. This signals an appropriate time to be in touch and find out if you need to do more work together. Sometimes it is hard to determine if the client is not feeling the new soul essence because the soul retrieval did not work or simply because the effect is not obvious for them.

There are many potential reasons why a soul retrieval may not be effective. It is possible that the person did not 'receive' the soul part and actively rejected it because of an emotional or mental block. If you are shown this on a subsequent journey, you can repeat the work with the explanation that this sometimes happens, while ensuring the client does not feel as though they have somehow failed the process. You may not have maintained sufficient focus and concentration when you returned from the SR journey, resulting in an unsuccessful attempt to blow the soul part into the client with full visualization of it flowing into their body. Again, simply repeat the work, paying particular attention to focus and visualization when retrieving the soul essence. Finally, the SR work may have been performed perfectly and the person just needs to do some journeying work to reintegrate and truly feel that the part or parts were brought back to them. This is your cue to assist the person with some integration journeys as outlined above.

The psychological expectations of the person must also be taken into account. Expectations can often be high, especially for a seriously ill client. Miracles are beautiful when they appear, however this is not the norm in the first session with a client. There is a distinction between healing and curing – healing may or may not translate into the physical body in shamanic healing practices. Shamans work in the spirit body, psychologists in the mind, and physicians in the body. From the shaman's

Section Four – Client Support

perspective, all illness is born first in the spiritual realm. Ultimately it is the Helping Spirits who determine the healing and provide the one that is most needed.

Because the effects of soul retrieval can be subtle, it is useful to ask the client to let go of their expectations and trust in the process. (This goes for the practitioner as well!) This is another reason it is useful to teach the client how to journey, to deepen their own experience of the restored soul essence. You can explain the potential range of effects that they may experience following soul retrieval, noting that subtle does not equate to ineffective. To instill trust in the client, speak with respectful authority and show confidence in your faith in the process. The client must also always feel safe and relaxed during the work. Your confident actions will psychologically assist in preparing the client to open up and trust in the experience.

Some clients, even with the best intentions, have difficulty in following through after the soul retrieval. 'Spiritual bypass' sets in and real world issues or chronic bad habits crowd out the integration work that they need to do. In such circumstances, you can work with the client to find a ritual to resolve their 'presenting issue.' If there is a lifelong issue or habitual pattern blocking them from doing the integration work, then you can both journey to find a ritual to discard this pattern that no longer serves them in their new life. You can help them understand what they need to do to fully actualize the returned power in their life. Your compassionate work will plant seeds of hope in the client.

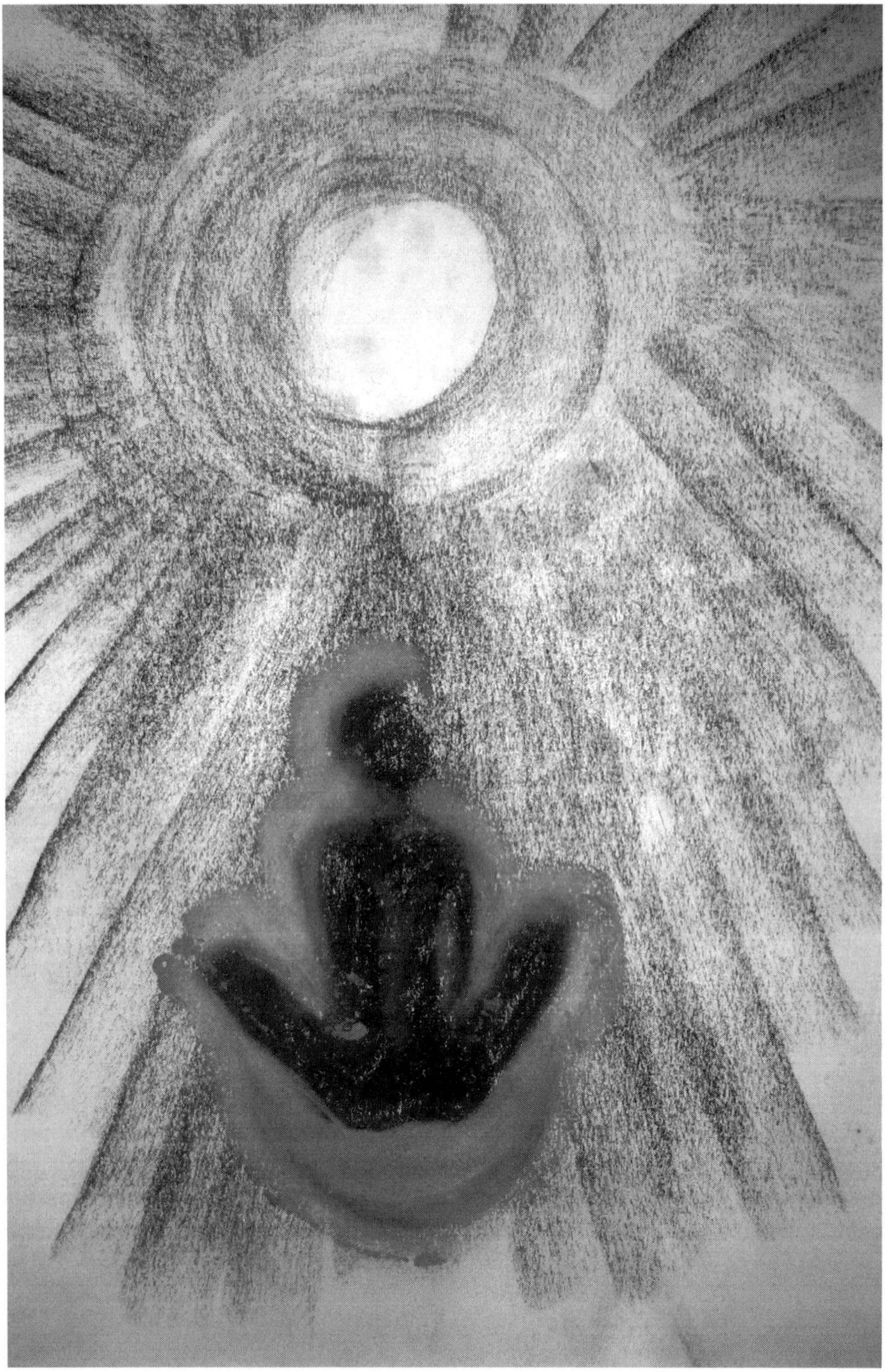

# Section Five – Advanced Topics

## *Other Types of Soul Retrieval*

This book focuses on learning the most common type of soul retrieval, the return of a person's soul part lost from some form of trauma. However, soul retrieval can also be used to retrieve energy essence, integrate, and restore the balance lost in many kinds of situations. As well, this is also not just for human subjects. Some other soul retrieval subject areas include:

- A physical body soul part (e.g., the energy essence associated with heart surgery trauma, or injury to a body part such as an amputated arm or leg).
- Retrieval of the land's soul where it has been traumatized by war or other violence.

## The Essence of Soul Retrieval

- Retrieval of soul parts of Mother Earth, which has sustained much trauma through the actions of mankind.
- Soul Retrieval for a family or business that has experienced trauma.
- Long distance SR for someone not physically present.
- Soul retrieval performed using a proxy.
- Journeying forward to select and retrieve an alternate future destiny for the soul.
- Past life soul retrieval to heal ancestral wounds.
- The retrieval of cellular memory to repair damaged DNA.
- Integrative soul retrieval for those who are terminally ill.

## *Alternative Methods for Doing Soul Retrieval*

This book describes the modern version of core shamanic practice soul retrieval as taught by Martha Lucier, who was instructed by Sandra Ingerman and Michael Harner at The Foundation for Shamanic Studies in the USA. In turn, their process was developed from the original teachings they received. Other teachers, such as Alberto Villoldo, Robert Moss and Victor Barron, teach their own versions of soul retrieval. For example, Villoldo's method of soul retrieval incorporates South American Inka traditions, while Barron's teachings have a distinctly Christian perspective and include a baseball-like wind-up pitch to push the soul part back into the client's body! Robert Moss approaches soul retrieval through the use of dream work. Alberto Villoldo is an especially charismatic and knowledgeable speaker and author. His audio series on *The Power of Shamanic Healing* (especially the section on soul retrieval) and his book *Mending the Past and Healing the Future with Soul Retrieval* are both recommended.

## *Opening to a More Complete Self*

An alternative method of restoring lost soul essence is a powerful energy medicine technique used in Quantum-Touch®. Quantum-Touch is an energy healing modality that basically uses chi energy coupled with intention and carefully controlled breath work. A trained practitioner can gather and present chi energy to a client at a high level of vibration so that the client can entrain with and enjoy the healing properties of this vital life force energy. The physical process of entrainment allows a weaker vibrating object (the client's energy) to synchronize with a stronger vibrating object (the energy of the practitioner). When one entrains with a stronger, more energetic vibration, one's own vibration is 'pulled up' to the higher energy level where it becomes easier to heal oneself in association with this more powerful life force energy.

However, in addition to this active or 'yang' method of pushing energy to where it is needed, there is also a quite different 'yin' process pioneered by Alain and Jody Herriott, instructors within the Quantum-

Touch organization. This more passive yin process uses energy and consciousness to effect healing. "Entraining to quiet rather than activity" requires a focusing of the practitioner's conscious awareness at a special point inside the brain near the pituitary gland. This facilitates an unfolding of the self, while consciously inviting a connection to the client who requires healing assistance. Both the practitioner and the client then entrain with this state of quiet equilibrium and unfold towards a state of balance and wellness. Quantum-Touch practitioners refer to this yin process of healing as *Core Transformation*. Holding conscious attention in the core point stimulates the brain and causes the unfolding process to begin. Breath work is once more the important agency used to amplify energy, ride it and effect change. Once a Quantum-Touch practitioner learns to hold their attention in the core point and breathe correctly with the proper intention, a number of different processes can then be applied to help focus and accelerate healing work. One of these healing processes is referred to as 'opening to a more complete self' (OMCS). Normally students will first learn to do the OMCS technique by practicing on themselves in the classroom. The exercise can then be done on behalf of another person who needs help with their healing work.

Alain and Jody's 'opening to a more complete self' technique in the Core Transformation II course is equivalent to the shamanic soul retrieval process (viewed strictly as an energy process stripped of shamanic metaphors). In the OMCS technique, the Q-T practitioner centers their consciousness in the core point and energetically 'wombs' the client's entire body, placing a field of energy around it. The womb is like a large 'rubber tube' that envelops the client's energy field. Then the

## Section Five – Advanced Topics

womb is extended upwards, adding a new section above it. The practitioner continues placing additional sections on top of the previous ones, ensuring that the existing sections of energetic 'tubing' remain open. Eventually the top of this long tube connects with the disassociated energy of the self, and this energy begins to flow down the tube and back into the client's energy field. There is a tactile sensation on the top of the head and in the lower Tan t'ien (i.e., the hara, the manipura, or navel chakra) as this energy essence pours back into the self. Additional work is then done to help the client integrate the returned energy and smooth out the experience for the client.

Alain Herriott explains the essential details of the process:

"After forming the initial womb you use your conscious intention to attract or 'tractor-beam' all the particles or pieces of the existent structure to the womb wall. You can think of tractor beaming as a 'Star Trek-like' magnetic effect that removes and holds to the sides any resistance in the client for the return of those parts that they had left behind. As the area feels open and free, then you extend the womb upwards all the while continuing the attracting of the particles within this extended womb. This creates a hollow or open space that is much like a vacuum. So when you connect the individual to their essence, it not only pours back in, it is almost sucked down into the physical form. It will come down into the body until it anchors at or just below the navel. You continue this pouring in process until the top of the womb collapses on its own. This usually indicates that the client has accepted as much of himself or herself as they can deal with at this time. Too much incorporation at one time may cause too rapid a change in them. While this is not really detrimental, it can be very intense."

The Core Transformation I course teaches the process of working from the core point and teaches techniques such as wombing areas that need healing. The Core Transformation II course builds on the basic core work and adds on new techniques such as the opening to a more complete self. Detailed information on the Core Transformation I and II courses is available in two DVD instructional sets and in a comprehensive *Core Transformation* book. The various Core Transformation I and II techniques are also taught in two separate weekend classroom courses. The current basic and advanced Quantum-Touch energy healing course descriptions and schedules can be viewed on their website at: www.quantumtouch.com

You may wish to research or experience other soul retrieval methods first hand to see how they differ from what you have been taught here. Several books and audio sources are listed in the section on 'Sources and Further Readings' to help you explore these resources. As well, you can check the Internet for information updates and new courses at Martha Lucier's web site at www.shamanismcanada.com or Sandra Ingerman's web site at www.sandraingerman.com or The Foundation for Shamanic Studies at www.shamanism.org

## *Empowering your Work*

Section Five – Advanced Topics

Everything you need to learn to perform the core soul retrieval process is covered in the previous sections. However, there are a number of ways that a shamanic practitioner can add power and precision to his or her work, using both archaic and modern techniques from other spiritual practices and energy healing processes. Several are introduced here; your comfort level and intuition will guide you in adding new techniques to your healing bundle as your familiarity and experience increases. Read about other energy healing practices and ask other practitioners about their techniques. Take the time to experiment and enjoy the ecstasy inherent in experiencing these powerful tools.

## *Guided Visualization*

Perhaps the simplest way to incorporate some of the yantra-mantra-tantra precision of Eastern philosophies is through the use of specific guided imagery and symbolism as reported in Buddhist doctrine such as *Healing With Form, Energy and Light* by Tenzin Wangyal. Culturally, this book's Buddhist beliefs have more affinity with the Tibetan and Mongolian shamanic traditions (which in turn are closely aligned with the ancient Bon-po religion).

At first reading, the text appears to be written for people engaged in their own personal healing work. However, a deeper reading illuminates the processes of identification, engagement, merging, and melting (like an alchemical or Jungian psychology process) with the powers of the five elements (earth, water, fire, air, and space). The shaman and the healer (the one who heals herself) are enabled to heal with their heightened awareness and the intervention of Spirit ("the Guests" as Tenzin Wangyal refers to them). Using a number of yogic movements, breathing exercises, and visualization, the author shows how to move the elements of the body back into balance, restoring health.

Wangyal's rigorous process is in concordance with medical studies that prove accelerated healing and reduced trauma from injuries when patients utilize specific guided imagery to envision the body returning to a state of health with the assistance of their 'imaginary helpers.'

## *Body Positions to Augment Your Journey*

There are also effective means available to enhance modern shamanic journeying. Felicitas Goodman and Nana Nauwald have researched the body postures seen on rock paintings, pottery, and other primary resource artifacts that appear to show shamans performing shamanic rituals while in trance poses. The authors broke down the details of these poses into a number of categories such as facial expression, arm and leg positioning, ritual accessories, patterns for accessories and body painting, etc. These various postures were then tested by shamanic practitioners to see if they did aid in the quality of shamanic ecstatic experience, and also to determine what type of shamanic work the pose was meant to amplify or invoke. By documenting the resulting journeys of

## Section Five – Advanced Topics

the shamanic practitioners, Goodman and Nauwald discovered the poses fell into several distinct categories, and enhanced the shamanic journey of the practitioner.

The results of this academic work have been summarized and redesigned for the layman and student shaman in a later work by psychotherapist Belinda Gore, who worked closely with Goodman. Her contribution to this reorganized material is the inclusion of important details describing the exact placement of each important journey element, and the effects or experiences that one might expect from the resulting shamanic journey. This author has used several of these postures for spirit journeys, death work, healing, and journeys of metamorphosis.

I believe that experientially there is a significant difference in the quality and intensity of the journey experience. It is remarkable that an alteration in body posture provides such an effect within the shamanic journey. The student must exercise attention to detail while setting up and using these postures. However, the benefits from doing so beg the question. If basic attention to detail and practiced posture changes can improve the shamanic journey, why are these postures and accessories not taught as a component of modern shamanic practices? Are we in too much of a hurry to pay attention to the details of our body pose, or perhaps too civilized to wear a three-pointed hat or paint our faces as is suggested by the rock art and carvings documenting the original archaic procedures? Practitioners are invited to explore some of these body postures as a means of journeying. However, it is also important to understand that modern core shamanism is based on obtaining information and direction from our own Helping Spirits, and not just by relying on archaic practices or the methods of other teachers.

Noted medical intuitive Caroline Myss makes a contrary argument aimed at western healers using shamanic practices:

"I prefer non-superstitious language. I like a language that is much more technical, because I think the western mind adjusts to it better. Shamanism is a first chakra skill, so it tends to use very earthy or occult language, which by no means invalidates it. That's simply the level of that language. The first chakra is the language the church would use and they would say exorcism, wouldn't they? Getting the spirit back from a demon. So it's the same thing." (DiCarlo)

In spite of this criticism, core shamanic practices such as soul retrieval do not have to remain labeled as earthy, occult, superstitious endeavor. Modern insights into the implicate order of the universe and the evolution of human consciousness by physicists such as Bohm and Pribram, ethnographic theories by Michael Winkelman explaining the neurophenomenological perspectives of shamanic cognition, and Arnold Mindell's psychological process-oriented therapy for working with the dreaming body all provide new food for the western mind involved in core shamanism.

Arnold Mindell is a Jungian analyst who believes that messages from the unconscious are communicated through our symptoms, sensations, and other bodily phenomena, in much the same way as they are revealed in dreams. Viewed this way, messages from the unconscious can be a part of Carl Jung's 'royal road' of individuation and personal

## Section Five – Advanced Topics

fulfillment in life. For Mindell, the body's symptoms are not necessarily pathological – they can be meaningful and purposeful conditions. The bodily symptoms are mirrored in dreams, and the reverse is also true: dreams can talk about body conditions. It becomes apparent that all of our physical gestures, communications to others, tone of voice, tempo of speaking, facial expressions, etc. are all mirrored in our dreams. Our physical diseases, problems in communications, and relationship problems can all be found in our dreams.

Mindell defines the dreambody as "an entity [within the psyche] which is dream and body at once." The psychological process of amplification is used to work with physical symptoms and makes dreamwork theoretically no different than bodywork; the therapist works with the client's processes sequentially as they appear. In this venture, the therapist's only tool is her ability to observe processes, and then amplify the process' channel of action in the body. Dreambody work also lends itself to working alone on oneself. Mindell suggests that using Jung's Active Imagination is an excellent means of dialoguing with the unconscious and amplifying dream material in this work. (Active Imagination is remarkably similar to the shamanic process of journeying.) For the client, there are several phases to the Dreambody work: self-exploration (becoming aware of a signal, determining its channel); amplification of the signal until a process begins; channel changing (e.g., going from feeling to kinetic movement); and completing the work by processing, integration and finding insight.

Given the wealth of new science that is applicable to core shamanism, science may empower us to find a path that discards the old

## The Essence of Soul Retrieval

belief in individual fragmented consciousness and seeks the perception of a world of wholeness, flow, and implicate order. On this new path with heart, one can exercise body and mind using Active Imagination, dreambody work, and guided imagery in order to hone the shaman's cognitive tools to diamond-like sharpness.

## *Practitioner Burnout and How to Avoid it*

As with any profession, a shamanic practitioner can end up feeling over-worked, under-appreciated, and wondering where all their get-up-and-go got up and went. It can sometimes feel like we sojourn alone down a very isolated road. Maintaining a high level of energy and focused motivation while doing shamanic work requires conscious intention and positive affirmations to stay centered and 'on top of your game.' However, the worst issue that energy healers seem to fall prey to is accidentally using and depleting personal energy while doing healing work. With nothing left to maintain their own health and wellbeing, these individuals fall ill themselves. If a person is unconsciously using their own personal energy to do the work rather than being supplied by the limitless energy of Spirit, then they are putting themselves in a harmful situation. It is important for us to remain detached from outcome – it is not our decision what will happen or whether the client will improve. It must be the client's choice to change and heal him or herself – we are just the conduits to assist Spirit in this work. Always stay focused on being the

## Section Five – Advanced Topics

hollow bone, in full awareness that our personal energy is neither needed nor appropriate – that it is only our ego wanting to 'force' a positive outcome to have the client see us in a positive light as 'a great healer.'

Endeavour to form a balanced and reciprocal relationship of 'ayni' (pronounced "eye-nee") with Spirit – a respectful desire to ensure that your work is accomplished with mindful appreciation of all the gifts received from your Helping Sprits. The Q'ero shamans of the Peruvian Andes embody this philosophy of ayni in their every action – nothing is done without heartfelt thanks and reciprocity towards everything that exists in their world of living energy. In doing so, a balancing of energies occurs, allowing both shaman and Spirit to work together in harmony.

On a more concrete level, drumming or rattling with intention, rites of protection, and a daily spiritual practice containing positive affirmations will benefit all levels of the psyche and help you maintain your centeredness.

Ultimately, as with any individual, you need to maintain balance in all aspects of our life including rest, variety and vacation. Make sure that you live a lifestyle providing nutrition for body, mind and soul. Your friendships with spiritual community and personal acquaintances are equally important. Seek out healing yourself if needed – the best shamanic practitioners still need another shaman. When all else fails, remember: shamans never take themselves too seriously. The world is to be explored, like hummingbird who drinks deeply from the nectar of life, and the coyote-trickster who seeks out adventure and fun wherever it can be found. Maybe it is time to have a talk with your power animals and get back in touch with your instincts.

The Essence of Soul Retrieval

## *The Delicate Subject of Payment for Your Services*

Finally, there is the delicate question of how much to charge for doing soul retrieval work. While your time, experience, and healing work all have value, how can they be measured? The question will arise as soon as someone requests your services. Some practitioners charge a fee, and some request a donation. Perhaps the best way to personally decide is to journey on the question and see what Spirit has to suggest. Ingerman discussed this in her Summer 1994 Soul Retrieval Newsletter:

"It really breaks my heart to get a letter from someone saying that the only person that I refer to in a 500-mile radius charges too much money and they appreciate my referral but it is not possible for them to have the work done. In my own practice since 1980, I have never turned a client down because of money. I cannot find it inside my heart to say to someone 'I will not retrieve your soul because you cannot pay for it.' I do not feel that I can make this choice for you, but I ask all of you who do not work on a donation basis or on a sliding fee scale to please search your heart and ask yourself if you can be more flexible around charging. I work on a donation basis and accept whatever a person can pay. I do not do shamanic healing as a business... I do it as a service. I realize how complex this issue is, and what I ask is that you search your own heart for the solution. I also believe that it is important to encourage people to do follow-up work after soul retrieval. You might decide to set different fees for the actual healing work so that you don't turn anyone away, and then alter the charge for the follow-up work. This is just a suggestion..."

*"What a strange paradox! Every warrior on the path of knowledge thinks, at one time or another, that he's learning sorcery, but all he's doing is allowing himself to be convinced of the power hidden in his being, and that he can reach it."*

— Yaqui shaman don Juan Matus, from Carlos Castaneda's *The Power of Silence*

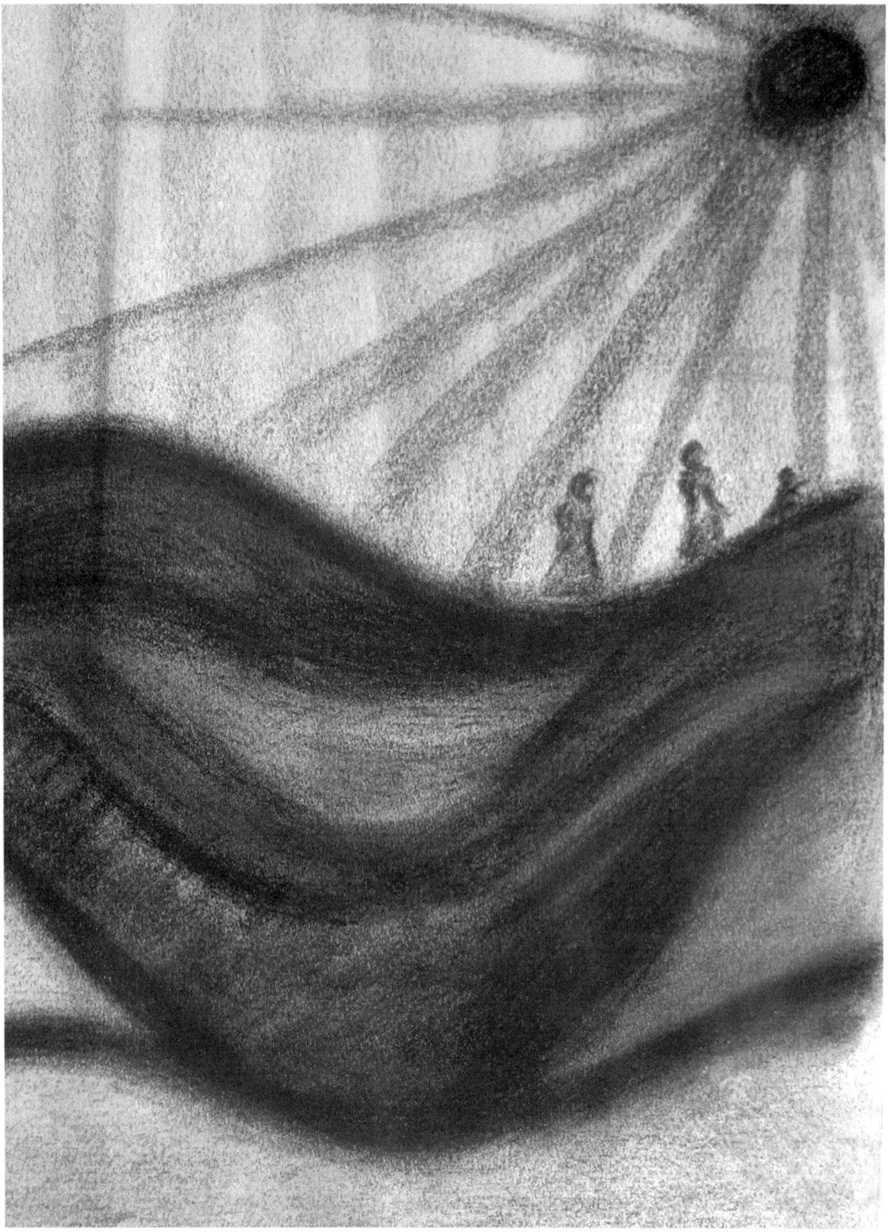

# Last Thoughts: Spiritual Aid and the Needs of Strangers

## *Living our Dream with Power and Intention*

Today, shamanism is often perceived by the public as a healing practice by, and for, individuals. However, this has never been the case in archaic forms of shamanism. The first shamans fulfilled a number of roles within their tribe: the divination of auspicious times for hunting, healing physical and mental illness, and acting as the tribe's mediator with the spirit and animal world. The shaman was integral to the survival of the whole tribe, providing the information needed to successfully feed the village, keep it healthy, and ensure that the relationship between humanity and nature was kept in proper balance. The failure to predict where the reindeer were feeding, a failed retrieval of someone's soul, or inability to deter malevolent energies from harming the village could lead to starvation, illness, and destruction of the entire group. A powerful shaman brought prosperity, health, confidence and psychic strength to the tribe, which is still exemplified within isolated societies today.

Today's shamanic practitioner is seen as an almost mythic figure of little value in our modern global village. However, shamanism's core beliefs of honoring the earth and walking the path with heart are ideas that humanity ignores at our own peril. A number of esoteric shamanic practices are clearly used to benefit all of society. Mongolian shaman Sarangerel defines 'eco-humanism' as the global aspect of shamanic work, and the broader application of shamanism to be the honoring of both our ancestors and descendants. Her vision of empowering the individual to provide medicine for the planet, as well as medicine for the healer, clearly shows how twenty-first century shamanism can impact the larger community. One very concrete and interesting community-based ritual she describes is the erection of a community prayer tree for world peace. In 'Medicine for the Earth,' Sandra Ingerman devotes an entire book to the role of the shamanic practitioner in the transmutation of personal and environmental toxins. Both these authors show how core shamanism is a force for positive change within modern society.

Seen in a larger context, our evolution in consciousness is driving a desire for civilization to sense our connection in a timeless implicate order, and greater awareness of the vital healing work performed by a growing community of shamanic practitioners and others who engage in energy medicine work. This new sensibility is supporting and renewing the role of the archetypal shaman figure within our society, and will eventually

## Last Thoughts: Spiritual Aid and the Needs of Strangers

lead to the honoring of shamanic work for the value it brings in healing the individual, the community and humanity as a whole.

Modern shamanic practitioners can empower themselves by learning important archaic practices such as body positioning and visualization, while also incorporating contemporary scientific insights in quantum physics, physiology, psychology and medicine. This may ensure that future core shamanism has even more vitality, performed with the knowledge, power and diamond-sharp cognition needed to heal the soul wounds of our mother earth and all her caretakers.

I encourage you to continue learning this 'lost art.' Remember that our Helping Spirits are the best teachers to help us on this journey and that you stand on the shoulders of those who have walked this path with heart for over 40,000 years. Thank you for your courage and willingness to answer the call as a shamanic practitioner and retrieve the soul essence of those in need. It is a vital service in our world today, where everyone suffers from loss of soul.

## *Feedback*

While many sources added to the scope and hopefully the value of this book, any errors, failures to grasp the nuance of what was taught, or poorly chosen words all remain the ownership of the author. I appreciate feedback on this material and any insights that would improve the next edition of this book. Send your comments and suggestions to the author at email address: ocelot.wreak@gmail.com. Thank you.

# The Essence of Soul Retrieval

# Sources and Further Readings

The following sources were used in the research and writing of this book. You may find some of these books, newsletters, CDs, DVDs and other resources of use in your own practice.

Achterberg, Jeanne. Imagery in Healing: Shamanism and Modern Medicine. Boston: Shambhala Publications, 1985.

Andrew, Ted. Animal Speak. Woodbury: Llewellyn Publications, 2005.

Bernstein, Jerome. Living in the Borderland: The Evolution of Consciousness and the Challenge of Healing Trauma. New York: Routledge, 2005.

Barron, Victor. Humanity's Spiritual Plague. Whittier: Eagle Publishing, 2003.

Bohm, David. Wholeness and the Implicate Order. London: Routledge, 1980.

Eden, Donna. Energy Medicine. New York: Penguin Putnam, 1998.

DiCarlo, Russell. Towards A New World View: Conversations At The Leading Edge. New York: Epic Publishing, 1996.

Drake, Michael. The Shamanic Drum: A Guide to Sacred Drumming. Topeka: Talking Drum Publications, 2002.

Duran, Eduardo. Healing the Soul Wound: Counseling With American Indians And Other Native Peoples. New York: Teachers College Press, 2006.

Eliade, Mircea. Shamanism: Archaic Techniques of Ecstasy. New York: Princeton University Press, 1974.

Goodman, Felicitas, Nana Nauwald. Ecstatic Trance: A Workbook: New Ritual Body Postures. Holland: Binkey Kok Publications, 2003.

Gore, Belinda. Ecstatic Body Postures. Rochester: Bear & Company, 1995.

Harner, Michael. The Way of the Shaman (Third Edition). New York: Harper & Row, 1990.

Herriott, Alain, Jody Herriott. Quantum-Touch Core Transformation: A New Way to Heal and Alter Reality. Berkeley: North Atlantic Books, 2009.

Ingerman, Sandra. Soul Retrieval: Mending the Fragmented Self. New York: HarperCollins, 1991.

--- Medicine For The Earth: How to Transform Personal and Environmental Toxins. New York: Three Rivers Press, 2000.

--- Soul Retrieval Newsletter. 1994 - 2000.

## Sources and Further Readings

Jung, C. G. "The Concept of the Collective Unconscious." In CW9i: The Archetypes and the Collective Unconscious. New York: Princeton University Press, 1969.

--- "Transformation Symbolism in the Mass." 1954. In CW11: Psychology and Religion: West and East. New York: Princeton University Press, 1969.

Mindell, Arnold. The Shaman's Body. New York: HarperSanFrancisco, 1993.

--- Working With the Dreaming Body. Portland: Lao Tse Press, 2002.

Moss, Robert. Dreamways of the Iroquois: Honoring the Secret Wishes of the Soul. Rochester: Destiny Books, 2004.

Ripinsky-Naxon, Michael. The Nature of Shamanism: Substance and Function of a Religious Metaphor. New York: State University of New York Press, 1993.

Roth, Gabrielle. Maps to Ecstasy. Novato: Nataraj Publishing, 1998.

Roth, Gabrielle. Sweat your Prayers: Movement as Spiritual Practice. New York: Putnam, 1998.

Sarangerel. Chosen By The Spirits. Rochester: Destiny Books, 2001.

Sarangerel. Riding Windhorses: A Journey into the Heart of Mongolian Shamanism. Rochester, Vermont: Destiny Books, 2000.

Sha, Zhi Gang. Power Healing: The Four Keys to Energizing Your Body, Mind and Spirit. New York: HarperCollins, 2002.

Sogyal, Rinpoche. The Tibetan Book of Living and Dying. New York: HarperCollins Publishers, 1994.

Storr, Anthony. The Essential Jung. Princeton: Princeton University Press, 1983.

Talbot, Michael. The Holographic Universe. Harper Perennial, 1992.

Tiller, William. Conscious Acts of Creation: The Emergence of a New Physics. Walnut Creek: Pavior Publishing, 2001.

Villoldo, Alberto. Mending the Past and Healing the future with Soul Retrieval. Carlsbad: Hay House, 2005.

--- Shaman, Healer, Sage. New York: Harmony Books, 2000.

--- The Power of Shamanic Healing. Niles: Nightingale-Conant, 2004.

von Franz, Marie-Louse. Projection and Re-Collection in Jungian Psychology. La Salle: Open Court, 1988.

Wangyal, Tenzin. Healing With Form, Energy and Light. Ithaca: Snow Lion Publications, 2002.

Wilcox, Joan. Keepers of the Ancient Knowledge: the mystical world of the Q'ero Indians of Peru. London: Vega, 2001.

Winkleman, Michael. Shamanism: The Neural Ecology of Consciousness and Healing. Westport: Bergin & Garvey, 2000.

## Sources and Further Readings

*"It doesn't interest me who you know*
*or how you came to be here.*
*I want to know if you will stand*
*in the center of the fire*
*with me*
*and not shrink back."*
— Oriah Mountain Dreamer, *The Invitation*

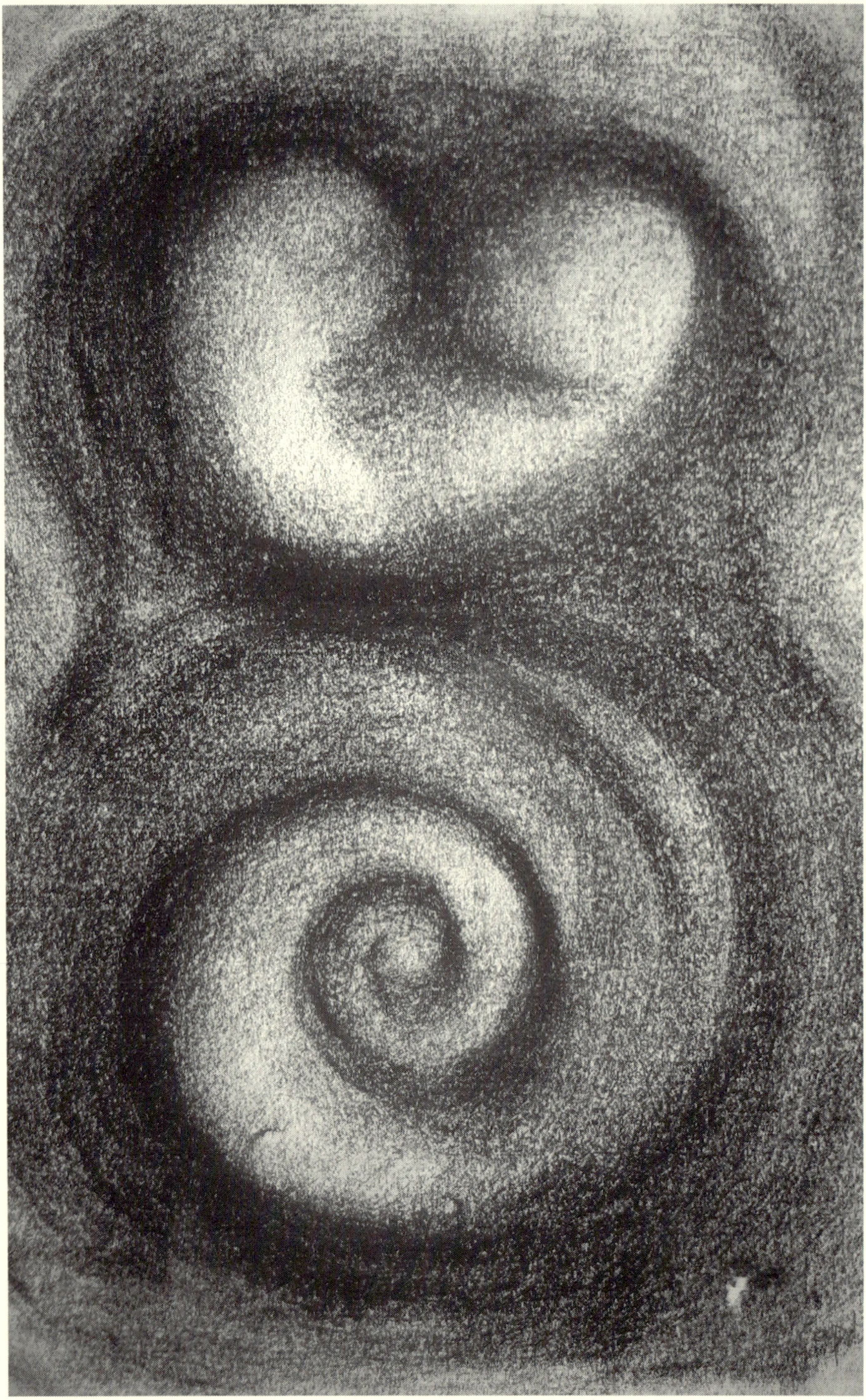

# Annex

Below are a number of documents provided by Martha Lucier outlining the various stages of the contact process with clients. You may wish to modify these examples for use within your own practice.

## *Initial Contact Message*

Hello Walter,

Thank you for your interest in the shamanism practice that I use to help clients in their own personal healing work. I understand from your message that you are feeling the need for a soul retrieval.

The first step in booking a private healing session is for me to journey to check in with my spirit helpers to find out whether they and I are best to work with the client. I need your permission to do this initial journey on your behalf.

Before meeting with a client in person I make several journeys prior to our meeting, to have clarity on the direction we are headed in. The client and I come up with an intention for these journeys through dialoguing. Soul retrieval may or may not be the healing process that is needed at this time. If you have a computer with Internet access, please go to this web page to read an article on soul retrieval:

http://www.sandraingerman.com/pages/2/index.htm

I also invite the client to journal their thoughts on several questions, to instill a commitment to the healing process.

As for fees, they range from $nn to $nnn per session (90-120 minutes for each session.) The session fees are only a guideline, as I leave payment entirely up to the client and what they feel they can afford.

Once the preliminary journeys have been done, we can then agree on a date for the healing work.

Please let me know your thoughts, and how you would like to proceed.

Best wishes,

Martha

Annex

## *Client Intake Form*

Hello Walter,

I am happy to begin the process by journeying on your behalf. I invite you to share what you are comfortable sharing as to why you feel you need a soul retrieval. What is not working for you presently? What do you hope to gain from this experience? What will be different after the soul retrieval? What are you prepared to do to integrate this soul part/s into your life? Take your time in asking yourself these questions, as they will help direct the intention of the journeys we do.

I also feel it would be beneficial for you to first learn how to do shamanic journeying yourself. In my experience when the client has the ability to journey, then the soul retrieval experience seems to be much more fulfilling for both the client and myself, as the client is more engaged in the process. I also feel that the healing work has a more lasting effect when the client is able to journey. I would be happy to help you locate potential shamanic journeying teachers in your area. However, you can still do your own search and take the time to find someone who you feel comfortable working with. If you are not able to find a basic workshop in journeying near where you live, then you can make a special appointment with me and I can teach the journeying work either in person or on the telephone. However, it is obviously easier and more powerful for you to do this work in person with the teacher if at all possible.

I'm happy to answer any further questions you may have. Thank you for connecting, and for inviting me to participate on this important part of your journey.

Best wishes,
Martha

## *Client Interaction Forms*

Hello Walter,

Thank you for sharing your answers to the questions I posed. I want to make sure I am hearing you accurately, and if I have not included something important or if you have anything more to add, please let me know, as this information will guide us with respect to our intention of the journey.

What I hear is that you have experienced …

I hear your readiness, willingness and openness to explore beyond your current belief systems without expectations. I hear your desire to experience healing through the use of the shamanic journey.

## Annex

One of the key elements in shamanic journeying is coming up with a clear, concise question or intention for the journey to the Helping Spirits. It is important that the question addresses the most important issue at this time for you. From what you have shared would a relevant question be: "..."?

I did a preliminary journey to ask my Helping Spirits if they/I are able to assist you at this time. In my journey I .... My experience indicated to me that my Helping Spirits can assist you in what you need at this time.

How does this question fit for you?

I look forward to continued sharing, exploring and healing.
Blessings.
Martha
......

Hello Walter,

Yes, we can book the private session for <date and time>. I anticipate a morning session to prepare for the soul retrieval, and an afternoon session for the soul retrieval. I think that our work together would be complete by dinnertime. How does this feel for you? I hear that the best question to ask is "..." I will hold this as the intention as I continue to journey for more information. I look forward to meeting you, and working on your behalf.

Best wishes. Martha

## *Follow-up After the Soul Retrieval*

Hello Walter,

I hope your travels to your ordinary reality home went smoothly. I have included in this email the recorded journeys from our time together. As I typed them some little fragments came making the picture more complete. I find it hard sometimes to give the full picture, interpretation of a journey, or healing story so soon after journeying (as I'm still quite in an altered state at the time!). I encourage you to read my recollection of the journeys and experiences we did together. Thank you once again for the opportunity to journey with you and I wish you all the best as you take the next step towards wholeness. Blessings. Martha

Annex

## *Teaching a Person How to Journey*

The practice of shamanic journeying is the main agency used to carry out shamanic healing practices. While it may be tempting to just tell people to read Michael Harner's *The Way of the Shaman* to learn how to journey, this isn't necessarily the best way to support a person's initial entry into non-ordinary reality (NOR). Journeying is a very personal experience for everyone, and we all have our own unique way to enter non-ordinary reality. Some people may be afraid of journeying for the first time and require reassurance that what they are embarking on is a safe and non-threatening practice. It is best if they understand the importance of being grounded and creating sacred space before journeying.

Generally, the practice of journeying is described as follows: the person sits in a comfortable chair or lies face up on a blanket, as though preparing to take a nap. An intention has already been formed for the purpose of the journey (e.g., "I am journeying to the Helping Spirits to learn about the meaning of my illness and how they may assist me in my healing work"). The practitioner then beats a drum at about 120 to 210 beats per minute or listens to prerecorded drumming music to help induce a light trance state. *The Beginners Guide to Shamanic Journeying* audio CD by Sandra Ingerman is highly recommended. (A rattle can also be used, which may enhance travel to the Upper World.)

With training, the student's consciousness then enters an alternate mode of perception, allowing them to locate an entranceway and move down a tunnel or similar channel to the Lower World. Once they have

## The Essence of Soul Retrieval

entered NOR, they can visit the realm of spirit to interact with entities such as power animals and Helping Spirits and carry out a predetermined intention. Occasionally the student may wish to do the journey while standing and drumming in order to interact with the spirit realm in a more physical manner. Special sitting positions can be used to amplify and enhance the journey experience. Standing up can also enhance the flow of energy.

When ready, a 'callback signal' is generally used to alert the practitioner that it is time to return back to ordinary reality. The practitioner returns to their body following the same route back up to our middle world of Ordinary Reality, and can then gently feel themselves return to their normal conscious body sensations. The callback signal can be demonstrated to the new practitioner so they are familiar with what it sounds like.

Experienced practitioners can describe the journey process in terms of their own images and feelings; new practitioners can be told they have the freedom to intuitively use their own imagery and route to journey to NOR. Some people enter through a hole in a tree or in the ground, some through underwater rivers, some see a tunnel and some people do not travel through a tunnel. Sometimes looking at pictures of nature or a mandala will assist in beginning the journeying process.

Anecdotal evidence suggests that modern shamanic practitioners probably learn and experience the process of shamanic journeying more quickly and effectively than our ancestors because we are more familiar with the manipulation and 'affective development' of symbols and metaphors in our thinking mind while in a meditative state. On the other hand, the archaic shamans of less sophisticated cultures, who still maintain a soul connection with nature, are more likely inherently capable of sensing the flow, connection to, and wholeness of the field we refer to as non-ordinary reality than modern core shamanic practitioners.

The type of imagery reported as the central agency operating in the shamanic journey experience is very similar to the 'Active Imagination' process used by Jungian analysts in the amplification of psychotherapeutic material encountered within a client's autonomous psyche. A client who has already learned Active Imagination while doing psychotherapy provides another way of explaining the process of journeying: "it's a lot like doing Active Imagination." This gives you another avenue for relating psychotherapeutic work to the student's journey process, and can allow the analytical psychology traveler to carry on a more active dialectical interaction with the entities encountered in NOR using their AI skills.

People can be encouraged to visit www.shamanicteachers.com or www.shamanismcanada.com when searching for a practitioner in their local area.

As a final note, it is not a good idea to let someone journey if he or she is unable to clearly distinguish between ordinary and non-ordinary reality. In such circumstances, it is better if you journey on their behalf to determine the specific healing they need.

The Essence of Soul Retrieval

## *Notes on Performing Energy Extraction Work*

(These suggestions were contributed by Martha Lucier for practitioners who are performing energy extraction work.)

- As practitioners we need to learn how to work with the energy behind our thoughts and emotions, and teach our clients to do this also.
- Spiritual Intrusion is a thought form while a possessing Spirit is a human who has died.
- Symptoms of Spiritual Intrusions include: Chronic neck/knee etc. Lung/Stomach Cancer, Chronic Anger, Chronic Fatigue, Chronic Depression.
- Things that are really lively have more sever symptoms.
- Intrusions are not 'evil,' they are just misplaced energy.
- Don't assume that there is a spiritual intrusion. Do a diagnostic journey with a power animal or teacher to see what healing is needed, and ask for an appropriate method to use to work with your client.
- Three Methods for Diagnosis: 1) Journeying through the Client as a tunnel, 2) Kinesthetic (feeling energy with your hands), 3) Strong Eye, journeying into the spirit body. (Some practitioners smell intrusions, others feel etc. depending on their power animal or teacher.)
- Merge with Spirit: if you can't merge don't do the extraction, as intrusions can jump into you!
- Method of extraction – journey for your own method of extracting, working with your spiritual helper.

Annex

- Prepare the client, letting them know how you work. Do not share the identity of intrusions. Make sure to keep confidentiality.
- Invite the client to release or cast away the intrusions as you are working. Give them a metaphor to work with.
- All Shaman's see/experience intrusions differently. What is repulsive to one is not to another.
- Be mindful of the seeds you are planting by the language you use with your client.
- After removing an intrusion, the empty space needs to be filled afterwards to prevent further intrusions or entities from entering.
- Have clients journey to ask a power animal to fill the space that was emptied (as a practitioner, do a power animal or soul retrieval) You can also use a glass of water to drink to fill space afterwards with intention.
- Do a ritual to make sure that you as a practitioner are clear of intrusions after you work.
- Don't fling intrusions around the room.
- Send intrusion back to nature, or neutralize intrusion with fire, earth or water.
- Make sure to ask for the identity of the illness as some things may not need to be extracted (fetus, pacemaker, Munay-Ki bands of power)
- Extraction is dangerous, as the intrusion can jump into you.
- Make sure to seal or close off the area where the extraction took place, to prevent something else from entering.
- It typically takes 3 days to feel the effects of extraction work.

## The Essence of Soul Retrieval

- It is love that heals…. not methods!
- Long Distance extraction - you need Permission.
- You can send a power animal to the person and watch the power animal perform extraction.
- You can find an object from nature and empower the object to embody the spirit of the client, and work on that object, making sure to dis-empower the object afterwards.
- Use rice to outline the body of a client, and invite the spirit body to enter and work with your strong eye.
- Do not tell clients to go off medications.
- Using Crystals: Quartz crystal is the only living thing that has the same identity in ordinary reality as in NOR.
- You can journey for clarity on cleansing and the use of crystals.

*"My heart soars like an eagle,*
*My happiness knows no bounds."*
— Chief Dan George

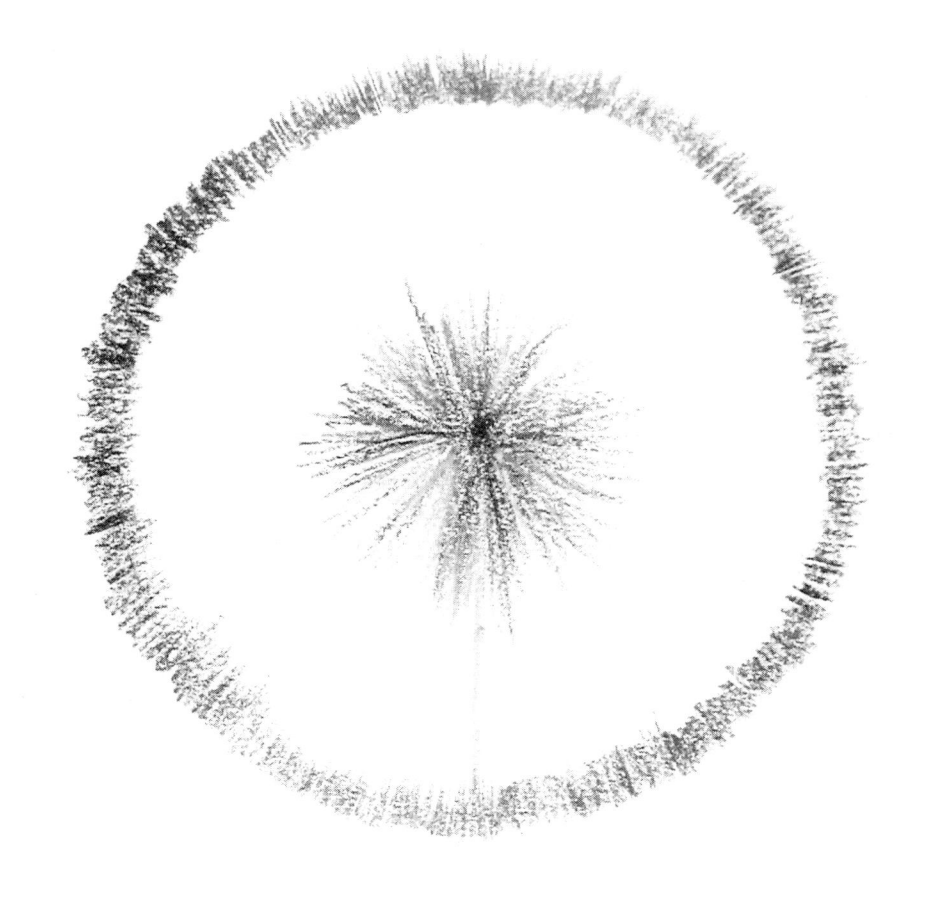

*"In the province of the mind, what one believes to be true is true or becomes true, within certain limits to be found experientially and experimentally. These limits are further beliefs to be transcended. In the mind, there are no limits."*

– John Lilly, *Programming and Meta-programming in the Human Bio-computer*, 1972.

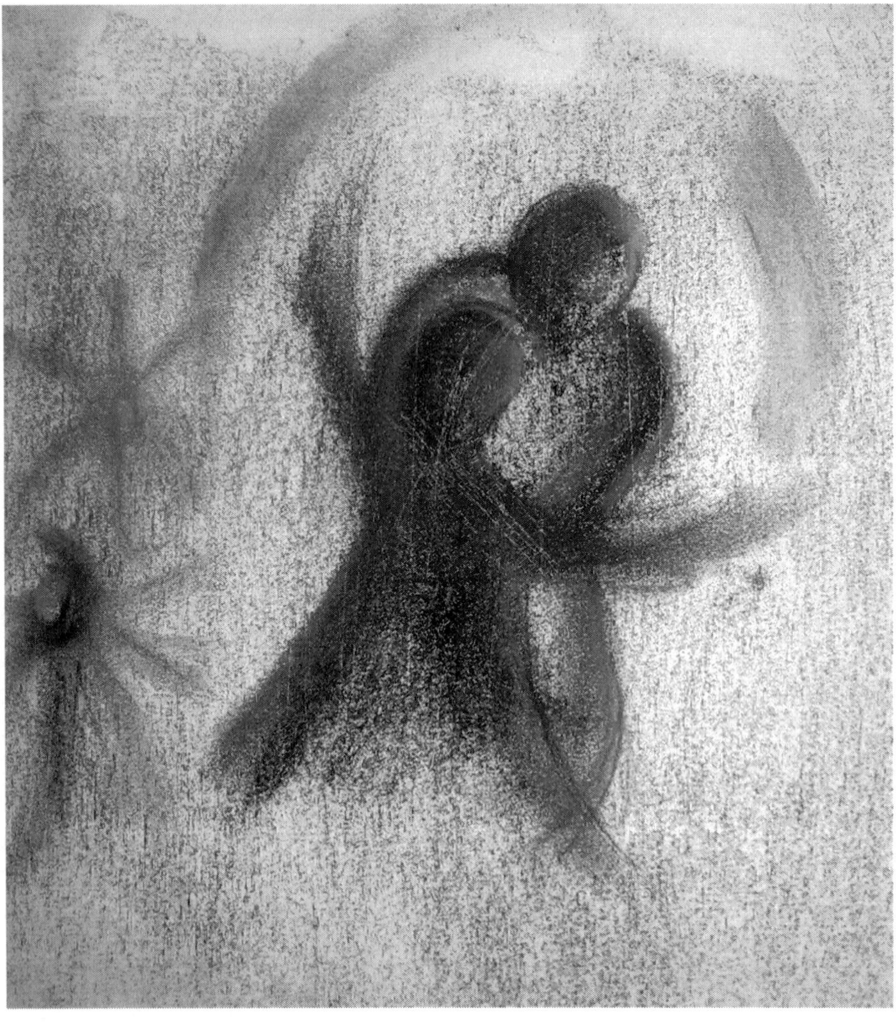

# Index

## *A*

Achterberg, Jeanne · 99
Active Imagination · 89, 90, 113
addiction · 14
affective development · 112
alchemical · 85
allegory · 67
allopathic medicine · 25
alternative · i, 10, 65, 81
amplification · 89, 113
ancestors · 30, 96, 112
ancestral wounds · 80
anchor · 59
Andrews, Ted · 66
    Animal Speak · 66, 99
apathy · 14
archaic practices · 87, 97
arms
    outstretched · 47
assistant · 27, 28, 41, 69
    female · 27, 69
authority
    speak with · 77
autonomous psyche · 113
ayni · 91

## *B*

balance · 10, 79, 82, 86, 91, 95
Barron, Victor · 80, 99
basic questions · 23
belief · iii, 13, 29, 64, 89, 108
better suited · 25
birth process · 38
blanket · 41, 111
body painting · 86
body phenomena · 88
bodywork · 89
Bohm, David · 88, 99
    implicate order · iii, 88, 89, 96
Bon-po · 85
boundaries · 2, 26, 29
breathing · 86
Buddhist doctrine · 85
business · 28, 80, 92

## *C*

callback signal · 50, 112
chakra · 33, 83, 88
change · 5, 45, 73, 82, 83, 87, 90, 96
changes in life · 73
check in
    14 day · 74, 105
children

working with · 70
Christian · 80
chronic depression · 14
chronic illness · 14
client
    interpretation of reality · 64
client intake · 16, 17, 28
client permission · 69
clothing · 44, 69
cognition · 88, 97
Collected Works · 27
collective unconscious · 13
coma · 21
commitment · 61, 73, 106
communication · 16, 17, 23, 89
    initial · 17
compassion · 4, 38, 47, 52, 65, 70
complementary · i, 65
conditioned space · 31
confidentiality · 28, 115
consciousness · 1, 13, 32, 33, 59, 64, 82, 88, 89, 96, 111, 129
    center · 82
contact · i, 21, 26, 29, 75, 105
conversation · 23, 59
core process · 8, 16
Core Transformation · 82, 84, 100
counter-transference · 27
crown · 53, 54, 55, 56
crystal · 49, 116

## D

danger · 41, 115
death · 14, 87
death work · 87
depleted immune system · 14
descendants · 96
detached · 14, 32, 90
diagnose · i
Dissociative Identity Disorder · 14
divorce · 14
do no harm · 46
doctor · 22, 24
donation · 92
dream · 45, 66, 81, 89, 95, 129
dreambody · 89, 90
drumming · 27, 32, 41, 43, 50, 62, 63, 91, 111, 112

## E

eco-humanism · 96
ecstasy · 11, 47, 61, 85
ecstatic experience · 86
ego inflation · ii, 13, 27
elements · 30, 85, 109
    five · 85
email · 23, 74, 97, 110
empathic · 50
empower · 30, 34, 39, 61, 89, 97, 116, 129
empowerment · i, 64
energy
    chi · 81

# Index

energy extraction · 18, 41, 42, 55, 114
entities · 44, 112, 113, 115
ethical action · 21
ethical dealings · 28
exorcism · 88
expectation · 76
    psychological · 76
experience
    own · 18, 77
extraction work · 18, 41, 42, 55, 114, 115

## F

facial expression · 86, 89
fairy tale · 67
faith · 29, 77
faith healing · 65
fee · 92
feeling · 14, 22, 51, 57, 64, 69, 89, 90, 105
    apathy · 14
    chronic depression · 14
    drained · 69
    empty · 14
    intense · 51
    numbness · 14
feelings · 23
feet
    holding · 57
fetus · 44, 115
filled with spirit · 41
follow-up · 7, 8, 9, 16, 18, 19, 75, 92

## G

gestures · 89
Goodman, Felicitas · 86, 87, 100
Gore, Belinda · 87, 100
gratitude · 39
ground · 18, 57, 59, 60, 61, 112
Guests
    the · 86
guided imagery · 85, 86, 90
guides
    spirit · i

## H

hara · 83
Harner, Michael · 80, 100, 111
    Way of the Shaman · 100, 111
healing
    accelerated · 86
    crisis · 9, 19
    process · iii, 5, 10, 29, 61, 82, 106
healing process · iii, 4, 5, 10, 24, 29, 61, 75, 82, 85, 106
healing story · 18, 61, 62, 63, 67, 110
heart · iii, 4, 5, 10, 11, 33, 34, 47, 49, 51, 52, 53, 55, 58, 59, 65, 74, 79, 90, 92, 96, 97, 116
helper · 28, 39, 114
Helping Spirits · i, iii, 4, 7, 8, 11, 17, 21, 22, 25, 30, 31, 32, 34, 37, 38, 41, 44, 46, 50, 55, 61, 74, 77, 87, 97, 109, 111, 112

# The Essence of Soul Retrieval

Herriott, Alain · iii, 35, 81, 83, 100
home · 15, 29, 39, 42, 45, 50, 57, 58, 74, 110
homework · 21
hurry · 87

## I

illness
    chronic · 14
imaginary helpers · 86
immune system
    depleted · 14
implicate order · iii, 88, 89, 96
incest survivor · 22
individuation · 88
inflation · ii
    ego · ii
Ingerman, Sandra · ii, 7, 15, 22, 25, 65, 75, 80, 84, 92, 96, 100, 111
    Medicine for the Earth · 96
    Soul Retrieval Newsletter · 75, 92, 100
initial communication · 17
initial learning
    your own process · 38
Inka · 80
insightful questions · 24
instincts · 22, 91
integrate · 5, 15, 18, 24, 38, 40, 63, 73, 75, 79, 83, 107
integration · 73
integration journey · 61, 62, 76
integration work · 19, 61, 74, 77

intention · 3, 6, 7, 25, 26, 28, 29, 30, 31, 32, 33, 35, 37, 40, 44, 47, 49, 51, 53, 61, 62, 65, 81, 82, 83, 90, 91, 95, 106, 107, 108, 109, 111, 112, 115, 129
    journey with · 25, 26, 40, 44
    of love · 31
intuition · 24, 26, 34, 44, 67, 85
invalidate · 23, 29
involvement · 24

## J

jewelry · 44, 69
journal · 29, 74, 106
journey
    preparatory · 41
    teaching a client · 10, 40
    unwilling to · 40
journeying · i, 7, 18, 30, 31, 32, 33, 41, 44, 50, 71, 76, 86, 87, 89, 107, 109, 110, 111, 112, 113, 114
Jung, Carl · 13, 27, 88, 89, 101
    Active Imagination · 89, 90, 113
    autonomous psyche · 113
    Collected Works · 27
    individuation · 88
    royal road · 88
*Jungian* · 27, 85, 88, 102, 113

## K

kairikai · 6, 7

# Index

## L

labels · 22
    psychological · 22
leg position · 86
licensed · i
life energy · 15
life habit
    detrimental · 75
life problem · 22
love · ii, 4, 10, 31, 38, 39, 47, 48, 52, 58, 65, 67, 70, 115
    not technique · vi, 37
lower world · 44, 62, 111, 112
Lucier, Martha · ii, 4, 23, 67, 69, 80, 84, 105, 114, 129
luminous cord · 46

## M

make room · 9, 41
manipura · 83
mediator
    with spirit world · 95
medical care · 24
medical intuitive · 88
medications · 24, 116
medicine
    for planet · 96
meditate · 30
meeting the client · 26
melting · 85
memory · 14, 65, 80

memory gaps · 14
mentor · 23
merging · 85
metamorphosis · 87
metaphor · 15, 39, 40, 42, 45, 52, 115
metaphor of receiving · 39, 40, 42, 52
middle world · 21, 112
Mindell, Arnold · 88, 89, 101
    dreambody · 89, 90
money
    additional · 75
Mongolian · 85, 96, 101
Moss, Robert · 80
movements
    yogic · 86
Munay-Ki · 115
Myss, Caroline · 15, 88

## N

nature · 13, 18, 30, 33, 59, 60, 74, 95, 112, 113, 115, 116
Nauwald, Nana · 86, 100
neurosis · 14
non-ordinary reality · 9, 10, 40, 44, 50, 68, 111, 112, 113, 116
not working · 22, 24, 107
notes
    important · 61
numbness · 14

# The Essence of Soul Retrieval

## O

OMCS
  opening to a more complete self · 82
openness
  state of · 40
original situation · 45
out of your depth · 23
overwhelmed · 59, 64
own experience · 18, 77

## P

past history · 22
past time · 15
payment · 74, 75, 92, 106
  receive · 74
permission · 21, 28, 40, 41, 42, 68, 69, 106
pi stone · 49, 51
planting seeds · 69, 115
possession
  spirit · 25, 26
possible complications · 37
Post Traumatic Stress Disorder · 14
postpone · 46
posture
  body · 86, 87
pottery · 86
power animal
  instinctual part of self · 47
power animals · i, 11, 30, 37, 46, 49, 64, 66, 91, 112
power object · 41, 49, 51

prayer · 31, 32, 33, 96
prayer tree · 96
preliminary information · 17
prepared · 24, 37, 41, 68, 107
presenting issue · 77
Pribram, Karl · 88
privacy · 28
professional · i, 22, 26, 29, 69
projection · 27
  and re-collection · 27, 102
protection · 4, 15, 27, 40, 91
psyche · 14, 15, 25, 27, 28, 67, 89, 91, 113
  autonomous · 113
psychological · i, 14, 18, 22, 25, 27, 76, 85, 89
psychological labels · 22
psychologically healthy · 25
psychology · i, 14, 18, 22, 25, 27, 76, 85, 88, 89, 97, 113
psychotherapy · 14, 25, 71, 113
PTSD · 14
pure essence · 15

## Q

Q'ero · 91
Quantum-Touch · iii, 81, 84, 100, 129

## R

rattle · 41, 55, 56, 57, 111
reality

# Index

non-ordinary · 15, 26, 32, 40, 44, 64, 111, 113
reassurance · 111
reassurances
   truthful · 46
receive
   willing to · 42
reciprocity · 47, 91
reflexive questions · 17
reframing · 64
Reiki · 19, 65, 71, 129
reintegrate · 16, 76
reinterpret · 66
relationship problems · 89
religion · 13, 64, 85
   Bon-po · 85
repair · 38, 80
   damaged DNA · 80
return home · 45
ritual
   for presenting issue · 77
ritual accessories · 86
rituals
   spiritual · 31
rock paintings · 86

## S

sacred · 6, 7, 18, 28, 30, 31, 32, 34, 37, 40, 41, 43, 49, 51, 74, 111
   relationship to · 25
sacred space · 7, 18, 30, 31, 34, 37, 40, 41, 43, 74, 111

open · 43
safe · 18, 26, 27, 28, 29, 68, 77, 111
sanctioned · i
Sarangerel · 96, 101
Satanism · 64
schizophrenia · 40
schizophrenic · 25
science · 89
seeds of hope · 77
self-importance · ii
self-knowledge · i
sensations · 88, 112
services received · 19
sexual abuse · 29
shaman
   archetypal · 96
shamanic journey · i, 6, 7, 9, 17, 33, 86, 87, 107, 108, 109, 111, 112, 113
shamanic mirror · 49
shamanic practitioner · iii, 2, 5, 7, 8, 10, 11, 14, 17, 18, 47, 85, 86, 87, 90, 91, 96, 97, 112, 129
shock · 65
shoulder
   outwards · 26
soul
   loss · 8, 14, 15, 16, 65, 70
   parts · 15, 39, 42, 44, 47, 49, 61, 80
   retrieving lost parts · 44
soul energy
   pure essence · 15
soul essence
   pure life force · 66
   returning · 41, 59

welcome home · 58
soul part
   impacted within · 47
   positive characteristics · 66
   rejected · 76
   release lost · 46
   traumatized · 66
soul parts
   other lost · 46
soul retrieval
   did not work · 76
Soul Retrieval Newsletter · 75, 92, 100
soul retrieval types
   alternate destiny · 80
   amputated part · 79
   cellular memory · 80
   family, business · 80
   past life · 80
   proxy · 80
   terminally ill · 80
soul thief · 46
special resources · 26
spirit guides · i
spirit journeys · 87
spirit possession · 25, 26
spirit world · 15
   mediator with · 95
Spirits
   Helping · i, iii, 4, 7, 8, 11, 17, 21, 22, 25, 30, 31, 32, 34, 37, 38, 41, 44, 46, 50, 55, 61, 74, 77, 87, 97, 109, 111, 112
spiritual bypass · 77
spiritual rituals · 31

Storr, Anthony · 27, 101
student · 9, 30, 87, 111, 113
superstitious · 88
supervisor · 23
support person · 24, 74
survival mechanism · 14
symbol · 45, 66, 112
symbols
   meaning · 66
symptoms · 14, 23, 88, 89, 114
synchronicity · 26

# T

Tan t'ien · 83
teacher · 2, 6, 8, 11, 38, 69, 70, 107, 114
telephone · 23, 107
terminally ill · 80
therapist · 14, 15, 23, 24, 71, 89
Tiller, William · 31, 102
time zones · 15
timing · 46
tobacco · 74
tortoise · 67
touch · 41, 52, 57, 69, 76, 91
toxins
   personal and environmental · 96
tracking · 37, 44, 69
tracking down soul parts · 46
tradition · 25, 26, 42
trance poses · 86
transference and counter-transference · 27
transmutation · 96

# Index

trauma · 5, 10, 14, 15, 16, 22, 23, 25, 28, 42, 44, 45, 46, 65, 66, 79, 80, 86, 95
   associated · 44
traumatized · 15, 66, 69, 79
trick · 46
trust · ii, 18, 29, 34, 67, 77
tunnel · 111, 112, 114
tutelage · ii, 11

## U

unconscious · 13, 67, 88, 89
upper world · 15

## V

verbally transmitted · 38
vibration · 30, 35, 81
Villoldo, Alberto · 7, 80, 102
vision quest · i
vital energy
   seal · 55
voice
   tone of · 67, 89
voices · 26
von Franz, Marie-Louise · 27, 102
   *Projection and Re-Collection* · 27, 102

## W

walking the path with heart · 10, 33, 96
Wangyal, Tenzin · 85, 86, 102
Way of the Shaman · 100, 111
welcome · 18, 39, 40, 42, 46, 58
wholeness · 89, 110, 113
Winkelman, Michael · 88
witness · 27, 29, 41
words
   mindful of · 64
world
   lower · 44, 62, 111, 112
   middle · 21, 112
   spirit · 15
   upper · 15
wounds · ii, 5, 80, 97
www.sandraingerman.com · 84, 106
www.shamanismcanada.com · 84, 113

## Y

yang · 81
yantra-mantra-tantra · 85
yin · 81

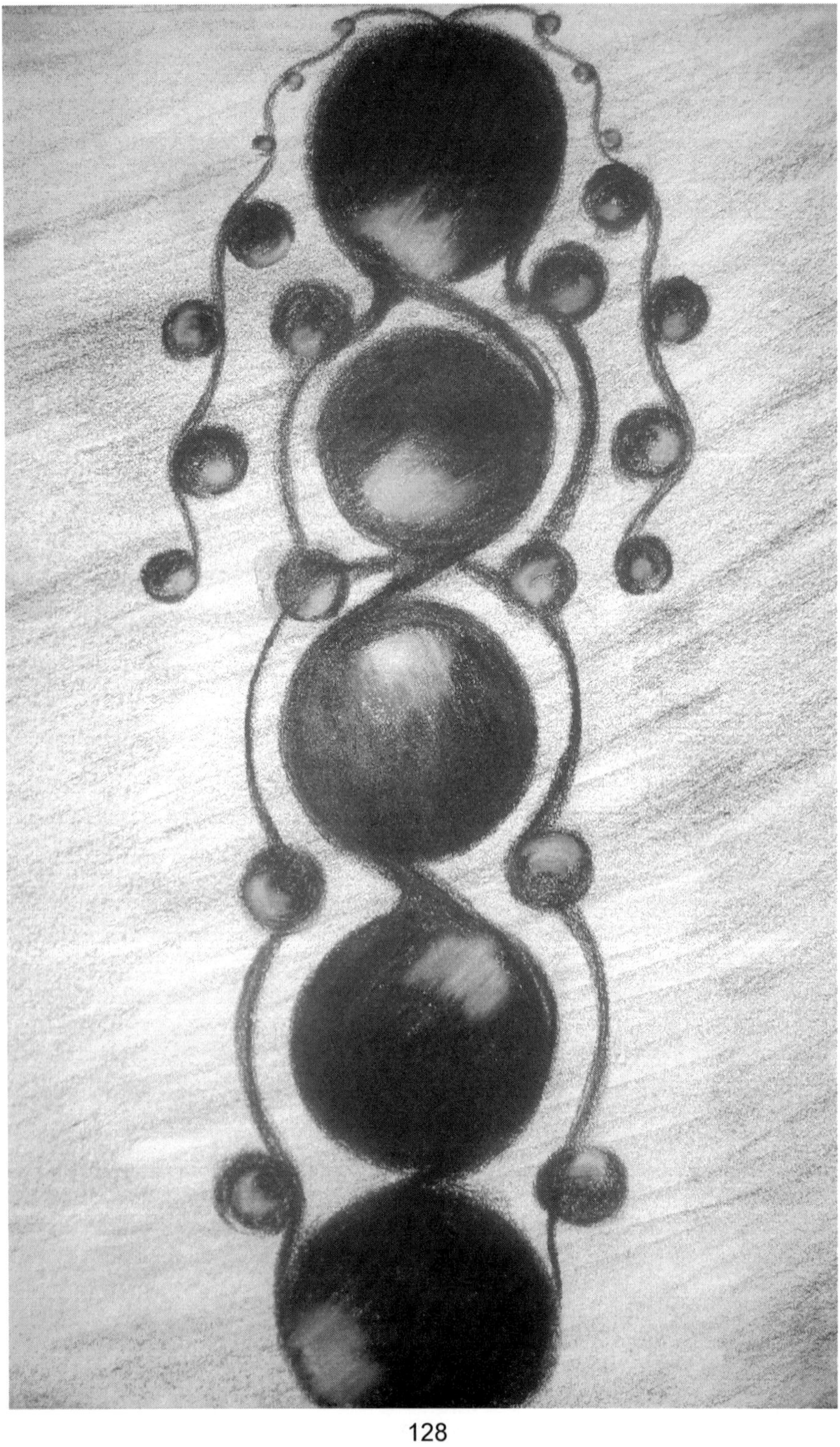

## About the Author

Walter J. Cooke is a Canadian core shamanic practitioner, Usui Reiki Master Practitioner and a Certified Quantum-Touch® Practitioner. He has had the great fortune to study with a number of shamanic practitioners including Martha Lucier from Canada, Mandaza Kandemwa from Zimbabwe, Angaangaq, an Eskimo Kalaaliq Elder from Greenland, and don Marco Nunez Zamalloa and don Martin Pinedo Acuna, both of whom live in the Cuzco district of Peru.

Walter uses a number of energy healing modalities and feels most helpful in his daily work by providing distance-healing assistance to clients in need. He has over 40 years experience in energy healing work, is a speaker at international conferences, and the author of many papers and articles in the popular press. Walter is passionate about his work and continues to learn new ways of perceiving subtle energy while applying intention and consciousness to health and wellness issues.

His heartfelt intention is to create consciousness that empowers each of us to manifest our most compassionate dreams and, with Spirit's help, to dream into being a peaceful future for all of our universe's inhabitants. In the meantime he will settle for altering this world one person at a time…

Printed in Great Britain by
Amazon.co.uk, Ltd.,
Marston Gate.